The
Friendships
of
Women

Look up Dee on the Web:
www.deebrestin.com
• Write to Dee
• See clips of Dee speaking
• Join Dee's webfriends for inside information
• See Dee's book and movie suggestions
• Purchase books, find sales

The Dee Brestin Series
From Cook Communications Ministries

BOOKS:
The Friendships of Women
The Friendships of Women Devotional Journal
We Are Sisters
We Are Sisters Devotional Journal

BIBLE STUDY GUIDES:
A WOMAN OF LOVE: Using Our Gift For Intimacy (Ruth)
A WOMAN OF FAITH: Overcoming the World's Influences (Esther)
A WOMAN OF CONFIDENCE: Triumphing over Life's Trials (1 Peter)
A WOMAN OF PURPOSE: Walking with the Savior (Luke)
A WOMAN OF WORSHIP: Praying with Power (10 psalms with a
    music CD)
A WOMAN OF HOSPITALITY: Loving the Biblical Approach
    (Topical)
A WOMAN OF MODERATION: Breaking the Chains of Poor Eating
    Habits (Topical)
A WOMAN OF CONTENTMENT: Insights into Life's Sorrows
    (Ecclesiastes)
A WOMAN OF BEAUTY: Becoming More Like Jesus (1, 2, 3 John)
A WOMAN OF WISDOM: God's Practical Advice for Living
    (Proverbs)
A WOMAN OF HEALTHY RELATIONSHIPS: Sisters, Mothers,
    Daughters, Friends (Topical)

The
Friendships
of

DEE BRESTIN

LIFE JOURNEY
Bringing Home the Message for Life

COOK COMMUNICATIONS MINISTRIES
Colorado Springs, Colorado • Paris, Ontario
KINGSWAY COMMUNICATIONS LTD
Eastbourne, England

Life Journey® is an imprint of
Cook Communications Ministries, Colorado Springs, CO 80918
Cook Communications, Paris, Ontario
Kingsway Communications, Eastbourne, England

THE FRIENDSHIPS OF WOMEN
© 2005 by Dee Brestin

Originally published © 1988 by Victor Books

Printed in the United States of America

1 2 3 4 5 6 7 8 9 10 Printing/Year 10 09 08 07 06 05

Cover Design: Greg Jackson, Thinkpen Design, llc
Cover Photo: "© Bananastock / Imagestate

Library of Congress Cataloging-in-Publication Data

Brestin, Dee, 1944-
  Friendships of women / Dee Brestin.-- 1st printing rev. ed.
      p. cm. -- (The Dee Brestin series)
  Includes bibliographical references (p.   ) and index.
  ISBN 0-7814-4316-4 (alk. paper)
  1. Women--Psychology. 2. Female friendship. 3. Interpersonal relations. I. Title.
  HQ1206.B73 2005
  241'.6762082--dc22
                          2005025735

To My Daughter, Sally

*At eleven years of age, your gift for intimacy
has blessed our family with immeasurable joy.
May you be strong, my darling, and open to God's
pruning; and may you so abide in Christ that
your gift flourishes, bringing warmth and
redemption to a cold and hurting world.**

*Sally was eleven when *The Friendships of Women* was first released. God has answered the above prayer mightily, as she now is a young woman using her relational and artistic gifts to bring warmth and redemption to a cold and hurting world. See Sally at www.aslanprints.com, and see the short video about the miraculous painting God gave her of Aslan (the Lion from C. S. Lewis's Narnia series) on my Web site (www.deebrestin.com).

CONTENTS

ACKNOWLEDGMENTS

How thankful I am to my precious women friends who have allowed me to probe their hearts and souls concerning their friendships with other women. You have struck a chord with women readers of all ages and cultures. They write to say they now realize they are normal to have the feelings they do. Special thanks to my "perennial" friends (season-after-season friends): to Luci Shaw, who gave me my start in writing, and to my now-grown daughters, who are using their gifts for intimacy so well: Julie, Sally, Beth, and Annie. Thanks to my late husband, Steve, who always believed in me and allowed me the freedom to fly. How pleased you must be, darling, to see this book continuing to impact women in a new generation.

Permission to use excerpts from *Song for Sarah* by Paula D'Arcy granted by Harold Shaw Publishers, Box 567, Wheaton, Ill. 60189.

"Perfect Love Banishes Fear" and "Salutation" from *Polishing the Petoskey Stone*, ©1990 by Luci Shaw. Reprinted with permission of Harold Shaw Publishers, Wheaton, Illinois.

Permission to use excerpt from *Being a Christian Friend* by Kristen Ingram (1985) granted by Judson Press.

Permission to use excerpts from "The Unexpected Gift" by Isabel Anders from *Partnership* (Jan/Feb 1984) granted by Mrs. Anders.

Permission to use excerpts from *Just Friends* by Lillian Rubin (1985) granted by Harper and Row.

INTRODUCTION

In 1988 the first edition of *The Friendships of Women* was released. The response was overwhelming. Women wrote saying Dee had touched such a deep need and had helped them to understand the relationships that were so important to them. They bought copies of the book for friends and relatives. Hundreds of thousands studied the book in small groups.

The principles in this classic are timeless, for Dee discovered them by seeing a pattern in friendships from Scripture. But applications to these principles may change as each generation faces new cultural opportunities and challenges. For example, just a few of the changes that have affected friendships for *this* generation are: cell phones, e-mail, the proliferation of "mean girls," and an aggressive gay agenda. So while the principles of God's Word are the same yesterday, today, and tomorrow, applications need to be updated for this generation's culture. This book is meant to be read for personal enjoyment, but can also be used in a book club for women or mothers and daughters. Discussion questions are at the end of the book.

You may also be interested in purchasing the journal that accompanies this book for your own personal study and reflection (www.deebrestin.com or www.cookministries.com).

A curriculum on *The Friendships of Women* is being planned for the future. You can check Dee's Web site (www.deebrestin.com) for updates. You may also join Dee's webfriends through that Web site and you will be informed when the curriculum is available.

CHAPTER ONE

FROM GIRLHOOD ON, GIFTED FOR INTIMACY

When Elliot Engel watched his wife and her best friend say good-bye before a cross-country move, he found that their last hugs were so painful to witness he finally had to turn away and leave the room. He said: "I've always been amazed at the nurturing emotional support that my wife can seek and return with her close female friends.... Her three-hour talks with friends refresh and renew her far more than my three-mile jogs restore me. In our society it seems as if you've got to have a bosom to be a buddy."[1]

*T*he clock radio clicks on, mercifully playing "Morning has Broken" instead of barking out today's market prices for hogs and corn in Nebraska. I shift under our electric blanket, curling my perennially icy feet against my husband's sleep-warm body. I peer out at the illuminated digits: 6:55 a.m. I hear our new puppy whimpering, eager to be lifted from her box, and the timed coffeepot gently perking. Soon we will all be up, showering and dressing for work or school. But for now, I snuggle down, hoping to enjoy a few more moments of the morning's soft darkness.

Reality breaks through with the piercing jangle of the telephone. My hope and covers are abandoned as I rush to still its persistent ring. I have little fear of evil tidings as I anticipate the voice of one of my daughter's fourth-grade friends. I am not disappointed.

"What is Sally wearing today?" Michelle inquires.

"She laid out jeans and her pink sweater," I answer cooperatively.

"Oh." Michelle sounds disappointed. "I was going to wear sweats. Is she bringing her lunch?"

"She's not planning to."

"But hot lunch is baked fish and beets today," Michelle argues plaintively. I ask Michelle to hang on as I discuss these vital issues with my sleepy daughter. It is decided: Sally will bring her lunch and Michelle will wear jeans.

Little Girls Are Closer Than Little Boys

When our sons were small, they had friends over frequently, but they seemed more absorbed in their activity than in each other. One friend, if he liked roaring up and down the driveway on Big Wheels or playing football, seemed as good as another. Never did I have an inquisition at dawn on what my son was wearing or if he was bringing his lunch.

Sally was much more likely to sit on her bed face-to-face with a friend, whispering and giggling. They were absorbed in each other. When Sally and her friend Gwen were six, they would often hold hands.

Sociologist Janet Lever indicates the differences I have noticed between our sons and daughters are typical. Girls, for example, tend to feel most comfortable with a single best friend; boys prefer to play on teams. Lever reports:

> There is usually an open show of affection between little girls, both physically in the form of hand-holding and verbally through "love-notes" that reaffirm how special each is to the other. Although boys are likely to have best friends as well, their friendships tend to be less intimate and expressive than girls'. Hand-holding and love-notes are virtually unknown among boys, and the confidences that boys share are more likely to be "group secrets" than expressions of private thoughts and feelings.[2]

Do you remember? I do.

When Donna Rosenow and I were in fifth grade, we took turns walking each other home after school, even though our homes were a mile apart. A standing joke occurred when we reached the door: "Now I'll walk you home!" Then we'd laugh and turn to walk the mile through the tree-lined streets of our small Wisconsin town. When we finally did part, our giggling and chatter resumed right after supper as we monopolized our respective telephones.

Girls are more demanding, empathetic, and confiding in their friendships than boys. They are closer. Zick Rubin, author of *Children's Friendships,* has noted: "Girls not only have a much stronger need for friendship than boys, but demand an intensity in those friendships that boys prefer living without."[3]

When our daughter was nine, her friend Gwen passed her the following note in school.

TO SALLY
   CHEK ONE—YOU HAVE TO

Do you like me????????????????
Yes, and your my very best
   freind ——————
Your a good freind ——————
Sort of ————

NO NOT AT ALL !!!!!!!!!!!!!!!
COME ON NOW TELL THE TRUTH!!!!!

I showed Gwen's questionnaire to our eighteen-year-old son, John. I was interested in a male reaction. He read it over, brows furrowed, several times. Gwen's thinking was so foreign to him that he had trouble understanding her meaning. When he finally did, he said, "Good grief! Who cares?"

We do. As grown women we have mellowed and increased in subtlety, yet we still empathize with Gwen's questionnaire. We care about our feelings for each other.

The marketing departments of two large card companies, American Greeting and Hallmark, would appreciate Gwen's note. They've been zealously studying women for years. Their surveys have given them a preponderance of evidence that women, like little girls, care intensely about their friendships with one another. Armed with this knowledge, these card companies developed extensive lines of friendship cards and e-cards targeted directly at women. With one of their cards I can tell another woman how much she means to me, I can encourage her when she's down, I can congratulate her on a job promotion, or sympathize with a divorce. You won't find a card line like this for men. "Men's friendship cards" would be a financial disaster.

Affirming notes are not just for little girls. Here is a note received from Sally's friend when both were in college. Sally is still receiving affirming notes from friends, as is typical of our sex! The following note from her friend Shelli Henniger was written in five different vibrant color markers, and Sally proudly displayed it in her room. I simply cannot imagine a similar interaction between college boys!

Little girls and big girls are closer. They are also crueler.

Little Girls Are Crueler Than Little Boys

Our gift for intimacy has a dark side, for our longing for relationship can make us territorial. Little girls, studies show, have a tendency to go straight for the jugular, often by making someone feel left out. "Patti and I were very popular in fifth grade, and we enjoyed the power of popularity," reminisced a forty-year-old woman. "Lynette wanted desperately to be a part of our circle. She would write notes to us asking if she could play with us at recess. Patti and I would exchange glances and then give Lynette either the thumbs-up or the thumbs-down signal." Most of us can recall experiencing or witnessing extremely painful incidents in elementary school. Rosalind Wiseman records the following incident in her book, *Queen Bees and Wannabes:*

> Mrs. Clarke, a well-meaning but clueless fifth-grade PE teacher, tells the girls to get in a circle for a game. Mrs. Clarke wonders why it takes the girls so long to get in a simple circle. The reason, which she fails to see, is right in front of her. Who will hold hands with whom? As the girls vie for the various positions that will display their social status of the day, Mrs. Clarke gets impatient and yells at the girls to get it together—now! And then a horrible thing happens. Carla, the most popular girl in the grade, happens to be standing next to Cynthia, the class loser. Will the impossible happen? Will Carla allow Cynthia to hold her hand? As their hands touch, Carla grazes Cynthia's fingers and then jumps away as if she's touched a dead fish. The other girls giggle while Cynthia also pretends it's funny.[4]

After his first years as an elementary school teacher, a young male told me how shocked he was by his inside look at the world of sugar and spice:

> I have problems on the playground with boys and girls—but they're so very different in character. The problems with the boys are competitive ones, involving a disagreement over rules or fair play. I step in, referee, and basically, it's over. The disagreements between the girls, however, become intensely personal. Two girls who have been arm in arm the day before amaze me by suddenly turning on each other and screeching cruel and revealing insults in the earshot of all. The wounds may not heal for months. Girls completely drain me. Give me the problems with boys any day!

Girls have a tendency, more than boys, to draw a close intimate circle and leave others out, hurting them deeply.

I'll show you the dark side of our gift for intimacy in chapter 3, as we consider the world of young girls, college girls, and even, sometimes, Christian women. We've become more discreet than we were as children: We choose gossip and betrayal over screeching on the playground. When one successful career woman heard I was writing a book on friendship and women, she said, with deep cynicism, "Those two words don't go together." Some women have been so wounded by other women that they no longer pursue friendship with their own sex.

Our depravity is deep, our needs for attachment are strong, and we need God's wisdom and power to overcome unhealthy patterns. But in Christ, we *can* overcome the pain, break the chains, and unleash a gift that will not only bless us, but generations to come.

Other women have withdrawn because they no longer want to endure the pain of parting—and parting is increasingly common in our times. Becky expressed it like this: "Every time I get close to a woman, she either moves away or gets a job. I feel betrayed."

Using our gift of intimacy may bring pain to our lives. But stifling it is not the solution. Kathleen tried that when she moved from Virginia to Ohio. She told herself, *This is it. I'm not making any friends because it's too painful when we leave.* "And that year," she commented later, "was the worst year of my life."

The scriptural models in this book will give you insight in controlling and tolerating the pain our gift brings. When God gives us a gift, He expects us to use it. And we have a gift. It isn't just evident in little girls; it is evident in women.

Women and Men

We expect our women friends to share from the heart, to nurture us with expressed affection, and to cherish us. We are disappointed, in fact, when a close woman friend fails to meet this high standard. We aren't surprised at all, however, to discover two men who are unable to be this intimate with each other.

There will of course be exceptions. There are right-brained males and spiritually mature men who are blessed with the gift of intimacy. There are also left-brained females and women who have been so wounded that they are not comfortable with intimacy.

Studies indicate that men, like boys, do things together—hunting, painting the church, or watching a game—but they do not often relate to each other as confidants.[5] Men tend to be side by side, engrossed in an activity, whereas women will be face-to-face. Men may confuse quantity of time spent in the company of other men with intimacy.

Ken, a man from Rancho Santa Fe, played golf with the same small group of men for fifteen years. When he gave up golf, he was dismayed to find he seldom saw his companions anymore. "I guess all that we had in common was golf." Reflectively, he added, "Our conversations, as I believe is typical of men, were at the head level, not the heart level."

Most men not only find it difficult to make themselves vulnerable to each other, but they are often uncomfortable being together unless their attention can be centered on an activity. One pastor told me that in order to have a successful function for men, there must be an activity. Fellowship alone makes them uncomfortable.

Richard Cohen, a columnist for the *Washington Post,* wrote the following sad reflections:

> My friends have no friends. They are men. They think they have friends, and if you ask them whether they have friends they will say yes, but they don't really. They think, for instance, that I'm their friend, but I'm not. It's okay. They're not my friends either.
>
> The reason for that is that we are all men—and men, I have come to believe, cannot or will not have real friends. They have something else—companions, buddies, pals, chums, someone to drink with and someone to wench with and someone to lunch with, but no one when it comes to saying how they feel—especially how they hurt.... Women will tell you all the time they don't know the men they live with. They talk of long silences and drifting off and of keeping feelings hidden and never letting on that they are troubled or bothered or whatever.
>
> If it's any comfort to women, they should know it's nothing personal. Men treat other men the same way.[6]

In the secular world, most men do not have a close male friend. When *friend* was defined as "someone you feel close to, see often, can count on when you need him," four out of five men declared themselves to be friendless.

Women are three times more likely than men to have a close confidant.[7] If a man does name a close confidant, he usually names a woman.[8] A young woman commented: "My husband tells me I'm the only friend he needs. I'm flattered, but I can't honestly say the same to him. I need the comfort my women friends give me."

In the Christian world, men who are involved with other men in prayer, Bible study, or accountability groups are more likely to have a close male friend, but they still rarely achieve the level of closeness that women do.

Ladd Wheeler, professor of psychology at the University of

Rochester, found that women and men are both less lonely when they spend time with women. The data showed that whenever a woman was involved in an interaction, both individuals disclosed more about themselves, and the interaction became distinctly more intimate.[9] Likewise, a study at Rutgers State University confirms that given the choice, both sexes would rather spend time with women.[10]

When I talk to my closest female friends, I feel my soul being sunned and watered when they ask questions, drawing out the deep waters of my soul, and when they empathize, rejoicing when I rejoice, weeping when I weep. I can't count the number of times my heart has been gladdened by women: an affirming e-mail, a heartfelt hug, a gift of my favorite hazelnut skinny latte (she cares enough to get it exactly right), or a green and thriving plant growing as our friendship grows.

God expects us to use the gifts He has given us! And most women have a gift for intimacy.

I have experienced some beautiful friendships with women, and yet, when I hold them up to the friendships of Scripture, I am humbled.

God's Friendship Pattern

A hole in a cloth seems small until held up to the sun. As rays come streaming through, you realize how great the hole is. In the same way, the inadequacies of the best of our friendships as women may seem small—especially when compared to the friendships of men. Yet if we dare to hold our friendships up to the light of the scriptural models, we realize how far we have to go. I want you to dare.

Insights for unwrapping our gift will be drawn from portraits from three generations:

- Ruth and Naomi
- David and Jonathan
- Mary and Elizabeth

I've included David and Jonathan in a book on the friendships of women for two reasons. First, Jonathan is one of those rare males who can teach even women a few things about friendship. But more importantly, I needed to include David and Jonathan to show you a pattern in God's Word. By juxtaposing these three generations, you will discover truths you may not have seen before. A design unfolds. If you've ever hung wallpaper or worked a weaving loom, you know the delight of seeing a pattern begin to develop. And when the pattern that is emerging is not on your weaving loom but in the Word of God, you realize that, through repetition, God is endeavoring to impress a friendship principle on our hearts. *God's friendship pattern can unleash and channel a woman's propensity for intimacy and help her to be the redemptive power He planned for her to be.*

Though I've considered myself a good friend, since I've been applying my discoveries from Ruth, Jonathan, and Elizabeth, my friendships have deepened to a richness I had not realized was possible. Scripture has also helped me gain insight into weaknesses I have as a woman. Insight can be a powerful tool to pull the weeds that are destroying our gift. This book will also deal with weeds of jealousy, betrayal, and lesbianism. (I realize some have picked up this book because they long to be free of the chains of homosexuality. If you are one of these women, I am confident the story of Rachel will give you hope and insight.)

To give you a preview of what is to come, I'm going to give you a glimpse of God's pattern by looking at just one of the threads that weaves its way through the tapestry of these scriptural models of friendship. In each of these three models, our Lord has zoomed His camera in on the meeting and parting of friends. Since these scenes undergird much of this book and were considered worthy to be recorded in Scripture, let us reflect for a moment on their value.

Parting Scenes and Greeting Scenes

When I am a detached observer of parting scenes and greeting scenes in airports, I experience a quiet joy—lovers lingering in bittersweet embraces, grandparents ecstatic over the first sight of a newborn grandchild, sisters hugging in reunion with unabashed tears. As I watch from the safety of my waiting-room chair, my heart is warmed.

It is much more exhausting to be an active participant; for it's in these most poignant of moments that latent emotion in a friendship boils to the surface. If we truly have bonded with a friend, then it is a tearing apart. It hurts. But it can also be amazingly sweet. As Romeo said to Juliet, "Parting is such sweet sorrow." There is a bittersweet satisfaction in realizing that it wouldn't hurt so much if we didn't care so much.

I was surprised by the depth of my pain when I put our firstborn on the airplane for college. I was weeping that day with abandon when my dad phoned from California. He was calling to wish me a happy birthday (which it wasn't) and was concerned when he recognized I'd been crying. But once he understood the reason for my sorrow, he laughed! Wisely, he asked, "Well, honey, isn't it wonderful you feel that way? Wouldn't it be sad if you didn't care?"

Each time my husband and I have moved to a new state, there have been tearful parting scenes between my sisters in Christ and myself. And though we as women pride ourselves on being able to express our love, there were several times when I truly didn't realize how much my friends cared until we parted.

When we were loading the moving van in Akron, Steve called up the stairs, "Dee, you have a visitor!" I was surprised to find Phyllis, a woman from my Bible study, perched quietly on a big box in the living room. Phyllis had never been to see me before. My surprise grew as she silently held out a beautiful afghan. For months she had been spending evenings crocheting this expression of love. Phyllis, undisputedly the most reserved member of all the women in the study, loved me! Spontaneously, I hugged her. At first her arms hung limply at her sides, but then she returned my embrace. Tears ran unchecked down our cheeks.

Likewise, when we moved from Indianapolis, I called Barb to say good-bye. I admired and loved Barb, but I did not feel assured that I was unique to her, as she is the kind of person who is incredibly warm and caring toward everyone. Because I was unsure of the depth of her feelings, I decided it would be less dramatic to phone than to stop by. To be honest, I didn't want to risk showing that I cared more than she did. But when I called to say good-bye, Barb began stammering expressions of love. "You don't know how much you mean to me," she sobbed. (How right she was—I didn't know!) Despite the pain, I was grateful for the expressions of love that would remain in my memory.

Two of the most poignant passages in all of Scripture are the parting scenes between Ruth and Naomi, and David and Jonathan. Since these models have helped me to realize the value of partings, as I hope they will for you, my attitude toward these painful moments has changed. I will not shrink from taking a loved one to the airport. I am so very thankful for the wisdom I have gleaned from this pattern. Since the original edition of this book, I have said good-bye to my dying father. I sat at his bedside for ten days, singing hymns, telling him why I loved him.

When I wrote the original edition of this book, my husband and I were young with three children. But twenty more years brought two more daughters, a daughter-in-law, and four grandchildren. In 2004, my precious fifty-nine-year-old husband, Steve, went to be with the Lord, losing his valiant fight with colon cancer. When Steve was dying last fall, he called each of our five children, and also our precious daughter-in-law, to his bed to say good-bye. Steve knew how important "parting scenes" were and said the words that will always be remembered. Annie, our youngest, shared:

> I crawled up on his bed and he just held me for a long time. We could just be silent together—I loved that. He told me that it was okay if I didn't grieve a lot after he died. [Yeah, right. I'll grieve the rest of my life.] He told me he wanted to be buried in his pajamas and robe to lighten things up a bit at the funeral. Then he just kept holding me, and he was crying. "Annie, I'm so sorry I have to leave you. I'm so sorry. I'm so glad I got to be your daddy. Annie, I will always be your daddy. Always. I will always be your daddy. I love you."

Those words are etched in Annie's memory forever, giving comfort. As painful as it was, as painful as it is for me to read them, *I am so very glad he said them.*

Though parting may be hard, though sorrow may be deep, it is not wasted sadness. Your presence may give comfort. Closing expressions of love may give consolation for years to come. The more final the good-bye, the greater the bleeding, but the more cherished the memory.

Even small partings can bring small comforts. I treasure those golden moments as a mother when I tucked a cuddly toddler under her favorite blanket with one last bear hug. Her sweet smile, her arm-spread "I love you this much!" linger in my memory as her childhood fades away.

And I have learned the most meaningful moments of a friend's visit may occur when I take the trouble to walk her to her car. The very act of showing that I care enough to prolong the visit often releases from her a confidence or expression of love that we both treasure. If I'm not willing to create these parting scenes, they slip between the cracks of time, never to be recalled when remembrance is sorely needed.

Greeting scenes can contain the thrill of recognition that God may be involved in bringing you together. Mary hurried to go see Elizabeth, because she recognized that God was giving her an understanding friend. Likewise, it's fascinating to see how quickly Jonathan bonded with David in their greeting scene. God knew what trials the future held for these men, so He caused their hearts to knit together almost instantly.

I met Luci Shaw when I was in my late twenties. She was a well-respected poet who had founded, along with her husband, Harold, a publishing house that did the first series of inductive Bible study guides, The Fisherman Series. It was with Luci that I published my first guide and with whom I became friends. I have the highest regard for Luci, not just because she is so gifted as a poet and a writer, but because she is willing to be a real friend and a mentor to those who are just beginning in the publishing world.

I interviewed Luci when I stayed at her home and asked her probing questions about her close friendships with authors such as Madeleine L'Engle, who is so controversial, but also so gifted. Characteristically, Luci shared openly with me, and I have many of her stories in this book. I was intrigued, for example, by Luci's deep friendship with a woman young enough to be her daughter, fellow poet Margaret D. Smith. This is how Luci described her "greeting scene" with Margaret:

> The minute we met, we bonded. It was incredible—I've never had such an experience.... Somehow she freed me verbally so that I could say things I never even knew I knew. She was a catalyst for me—and I for her. We can talk in a kind of verbal shorthand. We don't have to explain or fill in the gaps.

Being alert to the possibility that God may bring a person across our path will change our attitude toward first meetings. We may capture beautiful friendships that in times past would have slipped away.

Likewise, it is vital to be sensitive to the Spirit, letting Him touch our blind eyes when someone comes across our path.

When I first moved to Nebraska, I was desperate for a good woman friend. One morning, as I was going to a coffee for the mothers of new kindergartners, I prayed for God to lead me to a kindred spirit. When I walked into the living room filled with the chatter of young women, I prayed again: *Guide me, Lord!*

A pretty woman with an empty chair next to her smiled at me. Feeling welcomed, I went over, sat down, and introduced myself. Her name was Shell and, like me, she had a daughter entering kindergarten. We both laugh now at the memory of our somewhat awkward "greeting scene." As I'd been unpacking boxes in our new house, I'd been listening to evangelism tapes by Paul Little. When there was a pause in my conversation with Shell, I decided to try one of the openers that Paul Little had suggested. It was dreadfully canned, but I went for it. I said:

> I'm really interested in spiritual things because I've had an experience with Jesus that has changed my life. If you are at all interested, Shell—we can talk—if not, that's fine too.

It's amazing Shell didn't flee! Instead, after what seemed like an agonizingly long pause, she smiled. Quietly, she said:

> There was a time I would not have been interested at all. But my dad died last year ... and I have a neighbor that has gotten me listening to a man called Chuck Swindoll on the radio ... and, well, yes! Tell me how Jesus changed your life.

As it turned out, Shell *was* a brand-new Christian—but *so* new that she couldn't yet articulate what had so recently happened to her. Shell became one of my dearest friends and our daughters became just as close. Twenty-five years later, our daughters are women—and all four of us are quick to confide in and pray for one another.

Growing in appreciation for greeting scenes may also help us to remember those first precious moments. Christina Rossetti wrote, "I wish I could remember that first day, first hour, first moment of your meeting me."

Greeting scenes: How vital to *really see* as God does.

Parting scenes. How vital to seize last words, last thoughts, last looks.

These are just two of the threads in God's friendship pattern; however, you may be questioning—do women *really* have a gift for intimacy?

Are women *really* friendlier than men?

CHAPTER TWO

WOMEN ARE FRIENDLIER

We have found that friendships between women are deeper,
more enduring, and more plentiful than those between men.[1]

—JOEL BLOCK AND DIANE GREENBERG

*T*he July sun was finally sinking, promising relief from the heat. My husband, our daughter, and I sat motionless on the back porch, listening to the steady hum of cicadas, affectionately watching the antics of our six-month-old Springer-spaniel puppy. Unaffected by the heat, Effie enthusiastically chased a ball Sally tossed and carried it back proudly, tail wagging, eyes hopeful for a kind word or loving pat. Reminiscing, I said, "When I was a little girl, I thought dogs were girls and cats were boys because dogs are so much friendlier."

To the great delight of her dad, Sally responded, "Mom, I'm sure you would say something like that with a guy right here!" We laughed at our daughter's protective reaction, especially because Sally was unknowingly proving my point. Studies show that females have greater sensitivity to the feelings of others. This is one of many ways that females tend to be friendlier than males. Women are much freer than men to be intimate with their own sex: Women will confide in each other, hug each other, and express their love for each other.

When psychotherapist Lillian Rubin interviewed men about their friendships, she asked them why they couldn't put their arms around a man who was crying. One interviewee responded, "Aw, c'mon. I know you're kidding with that one." She assured him she was serious. He squirmed uncomfortably in his seat and said:

Men just don't do that, that's all; it's too uncomfortable.... I think there must always be some kind of fear about getting close to a man. We used to hug each other when we got together, but even that ... How can I say it? It was tight and self-conscious. You don't let your body go into the hug and the other guy doesn't either.[2]

Women Are Less Fearful Their Friendships Will Be Misunderstood

When Stuart Miller conducted interviews for his book, *Men and Friendship,* he found he continually had to explain to his male interviewees that his subject was not homosexuality.[3]

Likewise, C. S. Lewis commented that it has "become necessary in our time to rebut the theory that every firm and serious friendship is really homosexual." Men who wish to be close must certainly find this, as Lewis puts it, "a tiresome bit of demolition."[4]

There are strong similarities between the friendships of Ruth with Naomi and David with Jonathan, yet David and Jonathan are more likely to be viewed with suspicion. It is considered natural for Ruth to cling to Naomi, to weep, and to express her commitment of unfailing love in their parting scene, but men especially are intensely uncomfortable when David and Jonathan do the same things in their parting scene. Even Kenneth Taylor, in his original edition of *The Living Bible,* which is usually candid, dodged when he came to this scene. Taylor changed what the *New International Version* translated:

> David ... bowed down before Jonathan three times, with his face to the ground. Then they kissed each other and wept together—but David wept the most. (1 Sam. 20:41)

to the paraphrase:

> They sadly shook hands, tears running down their cheeks, until David could weep no more. (1 Sam. 20:41 TLB)

Taylor's later editions changed this paraphrase to more accurately reflect the Hebrew, but I smiled to see his initial discomfort at having men hugging or kissing one another, even in these extremely emotional circumstances.

Though some of our freedom to express love openly for one another has been lost, women are still much more comfortable hugging, weeping, and expressing their love for the same sex than are men. How thankful I am for this freedom. How many times I have needed this touch or expression of caring from a woman friend.

When my husband was so ill, and then after his death, there were so many times I would run into a woman friend and tears would spontaneously spring to her eyes. One woman saw me in the grocery store and asked me how I was. I started to cry and before we knew it we were weeping and hugging in front of the romaine lettuce and plum tomatoes. Women at church showered me with daily e-mails, casseroles, little gifts for our children, and empathetic hugs.

Once during this time Kathy Troccoli and I took some friends to *Women of Faith* and were seated six seats apart. Babbie Mason began to sing a love song to her husband and I fell apart. Kathy saw me out of the corner of her eye and immediately climbed catlike right over friends, from one armrest to another, so she could hold me. Just seeing her climbing toward me, with tears in her eyes, comforted me. As Babbie proceeded to her next song, "Standing in the Gap for You," Kathy sang it over me, continuing to let me weep on her shoulder.

I cannot imagine men being comfortable with any of the above scenarios for themselves, but for most women, we hardly give it a thought. How sad it would be if we could not continue to express this kind of love and comfort.

I've never felt the need to reassure a close friend that I'm not a lesbian, nor am I hesitant to put my arms around her or write her an affirming note when she needs comforting. I would feel "impoverished" if women were reluctant in expressing intimacy toward me. I have a second chair at my autograph table so that women who would like prayer can sit down next to me. So many women have broken hearts, and I am so glad I can provide physical comfort as we pray. I can hug her, I can stroke her hair, I can let the tears come, and I can kiss her on the cheek before we say good-bye. I can't imagine an American male speaker being able to do this, but I can do it, and I am so very glad.

Recently, our daughter Annie had her twenty-one-year-old boyfriend over for supper. I asked him if he and his guy friends were ever less expressive so that people wouldn't think they were gay.

"Oh, yeah."

"Give me an example."

"Well, when Eric and I go into a store—we make sure we don't hold the door for one another—in fact, we kind of slam it in the other's face."

I laughed. "Really! If Eric were really sad—would you hug him?"

With astonishment, David asked, "Hug him?"

I laughed again. "Well, would you sit next to a guy friend in a movie?"

"We would totally put a chair between us."

"What if you wanted to talk to him?"

"Talk in a movie? Why would we talk in a movie?"

"Ummm—to make a comment about the movie ... to connect."

"No way."

Why are guys so much less expressive together than girls? One convincing theory (embraced by Harvard's Carol Gilligan and psychotherapist Lillian Rubin) states that since the mother is almost always the primary caregiver of young children in nearly every culture, girls have experienced a deep same-sex friendship in their formative years, whereas boys have not. It feels very natural to us to be close to another woman, but it doesn't feel natural to a man to be close to a man.

If this theory is true, there may be hope that men's friendships will improve as it is becoming more acceptable for fathers in many countries to have an active role in parenting. It's heartwarming to hear a testimony like the following from a man in his second marriage:

> I never read *The Cat in the Hat* the first time around. I never diapered or bathed the babies. I just came home after my wife had them all fed and in their pajamas, and kissed them good night. It wasn't macho to really mother them. Now the rules have changed. Real men take care of their kids. I like that.[5]

Women Know How to Volley in Conversation

One woman asked, "How come there's no give-and-take in a conversation with a man? Sometimes it's like trying to play tennis with no one in the other court."[6]

Deborah Tannen, linguist, and author of the best-selling *You Just*

Don't Understand: Women and Men in Conversation, says that when men and women talk to one another, they are engaging in "cross-cultural" communication. Men excel in what Tannen calls "report talk," where they monologue; whereas women excel in "rapport-talk," where they volley in conversation. The essence of women's friendships, Tannen says, is talk, "a language of rapport: a way of establishing connections and negotiating relationships…. For most men, talk is primarily a means to preserve independence and negotiate and maintain status in a hierarchal social order. This is done by exhibiting knowledge and skill, and by holding center stage through verbal performance such as story-telling, joking, or imparting information."[7]

Samantha, a bright twelve-year-old from Maryland, amused me when she said,

> If I want to have a conversation that's not totally one-sided, I talk
> to girls—because girls know how to listen and respond. That's an
> important quality—and boys don't have it.

My daughter Sally's husband is an FBI agent. When they were dating, Sally was longing for more of a volley in their conversations, especially when their relationship was long distance and they communicated almost exclusively by phone. She sometimes wondered if he was really listening to her. She said:

"I'd love it, Phil, if you could ask me more questions when I'm talking. Or, if not questions, just some verbal affirmation."

"Can you give me an example?"

"Like: 'mm-hmm,' 'yeah,' or just any kind of noise so that I know you are there!"

Phillip then asked a couple of male FBI agents how they would feel if he responded like that while they were talking.

"I'd think you weren't listening."

"I'd think you were gay."

How different we are.

There are males who, without coaching, know how to volley, how to ask questions, and how to respond to feelings. Jonathan was one. My husband was another. But the comment I made to my college roommates about Steve when I met him was, "This is the first time I've been able to communicate with a guy the way I can communicate with my girlfriends."

When our left-brained son John was in high school, I tried to teach him how to draw people out in conversation. John is charming, good-looking, and athletic—and in high school the teenage girls flocked around him. But I remember teasing him, noting that it was the girls who did most of the listening. I know this is not unusual in relationships between men and women. Most women will tell you that in their friendships with men, they listen, they draw out with questions, they affirm and encourage.

I wanted John to break free of this male mode, to be able, like Christ, to draw others out with questions. I've quoted to him the verse: "The purposes of a man's heart are deep waters, but a man of understanding draws them out" (Prov. 20:5). So I engaged our son in a game, to which he reluctantly agreed.

"John," I began, "pretend I'm the new girl at school. Ask me questions that call for more than a one-word answer."

John eyed me with suspicion, but he good-naturedly cooperated: "Hi, good-lookin'!" He put his arm around me and winked. "What's your name?"

I stiffened. "Alice Smith."

"Where do you live, Alice?"

"902 Elm Street," I replied.

Giving me an exasperated look that implied I was the problem, John made one final attempt. "What's your favorite subject?"

"Math."

"Mom! You're just giving me a hard time!"

"Don't give up!" I pleaded. "With this last question, you're getting somewhere. Now pursue your thought. Ask Alice why she likes math, what it is about math that intrigues her!"

Now John was smiling. "I'm not really sure I care why Alice likes math."

"Aha!" I said, judgmentally.

Although John labeled my conclusion chauvinistic, I believe the evidence is mounting that women, from infancy on, are better equipped to care about others.

Women's Brains Function Differently

Scientists have discovered differences between the brain functions of men and women. We actually think differently than men. (My ninety-three-year-old mother said: "I could have told them that!") Neurologists first began to suspect this when they noticed that males experienced a greater loss of function after a stroke than females. In the years since the first printing of this book, the evidence for biology having a strong role in our differences has steadily mounted. An article in *Scientific American* states:

> For the past few decades, it has been ideologically fashionable to insist that these behavioral differences are minimal and are the consequence of *variations in experience* during development before and after adolescence.[8]

However, the article explains, accumulating evidence instead reveals *great* differences in the sexes from infancy on, so those differences are *best explained* by "differently wired brains ..."[9]

At the end of the twentieth century it was politically correct to believe the sexes were androgynous and that men and women were therefore equally interested and talented at the same tasks. During this time, Sweden invested in a massive advertising campaign to encourage fathers to take care of their children. Maternal leave was changed to parental leave. Yet, most fathers did not take leave, and among those who did, traditional parenting styles still emerged. The "mothers displayed affectionate behavior, vocalized, smiled, tended, held, disciplined, and soothed the infant more than the fathers did."[10]

When it became harder to maintain that fathers were just as nurturing as mothers, the politically correct belief was that it was because our culture made us that way. Yet studies reveal that nurturing differences are evident from very early ages. Two-year-old girls like dolls and play at parenting more than boys do.[11] Four-year-old boys asked to watch a baby watch it passively. Four-year-old girls tend to do it actively.[12] (Mothers of toddlers around the world are thinking, *Do we really need studies to prove that God wired boys and girls differently? Just spend an hour at my house, hut, or igloo!)*

Our brains have a left and right side, like a walnut. It is almost as if we have two minds; each hemisphere can operate independently of the other. Each side has its own distinctive strengths. Simplistically put, the left hemisphere is logical and interested in detail; the right hemisphere is creative and interested in the unbounded aspects of the world such as people and emotions. Both men and women tend to be left-brain dominant, but there is increasing scientific evidence that women seem to be less handicapped in the use of the right brain.[13] This is because women seem to think through both hemispheres, whereas men's brains are more lateralized; that is, they think strongly through the left or right side (usually the left).[14]

One theory explaining this difference is related to the communicating link *(the corpus callosum).* Dr. Donald Joy, in an interview with Dr. James Dobson, explained that it seems a male's communicating link is damaged prenatally through a chemical androgen wash. "Males simply cannot talk to themselves back and forth between the hemispheres the way that a woman can."[15] Because a woman tends to use both hemispheres, one can compensate for the other's loss.

I am certainly not trying to disparage the male brain! There are some definite advantages when one hemisphere does not hamper the other hemisphere. The goal-oriented left hemisphere sets out to solve problems and often does very well, being undistracted by the relational right hemisphere. However, our differences can cause frustration between the sexes.

Marriage counselor Gary Smalley tells of shopping with his wife. She said she wanted to buy a blouse, so Gary's left brain zeroed in on the problem. ("I wanted to conquer the blouse!") But while they were shopping, his wife didn't really seem that interested in the problem. She was looking at other things and even suggested they sit down and have coffee together! She kept interrupting "the hunt!"[16]

For the small percentage of men who are right-brained (sometimes, but not necessarily, those men who are left-handed; often those who are intensely interested in music, arts, or humanities), they are *very* right-brained: sensitive, in touch with feelings and with people. Later I'll make a case for David and Jonathan being right-brained and therefore equipped to teach us women a few things about friendship.

But most men are handicapped in the use of the right hemisphere and, correspondingly, in the perception of emotions and of people—two strengths of the right hemisphere.[17]

One pastor introduced me before I spoke as "the woman who said I used half my brain!" Let me make it clear that I believe that both males and females are fearfully and wonderfully made! There are strengths in thinking globally, as most women do, and strengths in thinking laterally, as most men do. One strength that left-brained men seem to have is the desire to solve problems. One strength that right-brained men seem to have is to be particularly good marksmen. In Judges 20:16 we are told,

> Among all these soldiers there were seven hundred chosen men
> who were left-handed, each of whom could sling a stone at a hair
> and not miss.

Far be it for me to disagree with the Creator of the universe in how He designed us! Scripture makes it clear that both sexes are made in the image of God, and yet they are different: male and female (Gen. 1:27).

Women Are Less Handicapped in the Perception of Emotions

The right side of the brain perceives emotions. Therefore, women, who use both hemispheres, are better at getting in touch with feelings. *Parents* magazine cited a study showing that "in the cradle, girl infants are more likely than boy babies to cry (as if in sympathy) when they hear other babies cry."[18] Karen made this comment: "My husband, Sid, is great, but when we move to a new town, I crave a woman friend because a woman can get in touch with my feelings." A man is apt to give you a one-two-three solution to a problem, whereas a woman will empathize.

There is also evidence that the right side of the brain helps in the expression of emotion. Neurologist Elliot Ross of the University of Texas discovered that damage to a particular region of the right hemisphere impairs our ability to express or interpret what we feel, producing what he has labeled *aprodosia*.[19] We've always assumed that the reason men don't cry is cultural, but there may, in fact, be underlying biological factors.

Women Are Less Handicapped in the Perception of Persons

Another strength of the right hemisphere is the perception of persons. The Swiss physician Paul Tournier calls this "a sense of the person." Perhaps this is what gave Mary of Bethany the sensitivity to come to Jesus with a jar of expensive perfume and anoint His head in sympathetic preparation for His burial. The men were shocked at the "waste," but Mary valued the person, and Jesus said, "I tell you the truth, wherever this gospel is preached throughout the world, what she has done will also be told, in memory of her" (Matt. 26:13).

When I think about how that fragrance clung to Jesus during the next week—through the beatings, as He carried His cross, and as He hung there in agony—I am so thankful to Mary for using her gift for intimacy in obedience to the leading of the Spirit.

Paul Tournier asks, "Who is it who remembers people's birthdays? Women more than men."[20] Tournier tells of how his wife, Nelly, because of her "sense of person," transformed the medical meetings of which he was in charge:

> It was the extreme care and interest she showed toward each participant that helped create the personal atmosphere.... In any other medical conference only ideas matter, and the delegates are appreciated only in terms of their scientific input. But in the Bossey meetings everyone was made welcome and was valued as a person.[21]

After Nelly's death, her influence continued. The meetings "almost entirely abandoned the old tradition of master lectures, so as to be able to devote time to the personal experiences and problems of the delegates." Nelly's gift for friendship is seeing multiplied results.[22]

The kind of small discussion group that I prefer is one in which each member feels valued. I want the discussion leader to curtail his own tendency to talk and seriously attempt to draw out those in the group. I want him to be alert to each member's facial expression and occasionally to go around the whole group asking for individual feelings or personal applications.

I am intensely frustrated by a group—and it happens much more frequently with a man at the helm—that seems to ignore the members and concentrates exclusively on the lesson. I *do* want to study the lesson (and I confess I have observed many women's groups that don't), but I don't want the study of the lesson to supersede the needs of the people. When I am in a group like this, I have to repress an urge to stand and scream: "THESE PEOPLE ARE NOT FEELING VALUED! THEY ARE GOING TO LEAVE THIS ROOM FEELING AS IF THEIR PRESENCE DIDN'T MATTER!"

Again, there are abundant studies that show that a female's sense of the person is evident from a very early age. Studies performed on babies as young as one day old have shown that girls stare longer at human faces than at mechanical objects, while boys do just the opposite.[23] Preschool boys are more likely to draw objects, and preschool girls, people.[24] Studies at Harvard have found that "girl babies recognize individual human faces and distinguish between voices before male babies of the same age."[25] Another study found that:

> At four months a boy will react to an inanimate object as readily as to a person. Given the choice between a mother's face and a bright geometric object hanging over the crib, the boy, unlike the girl, will just as frequently babble at the inanimate object as at his mother.[26]

When our sons were babies, we enjoyed watching them on their backs in their cribs, arms and legs excitedly flailing over a brightly painted mobile. Since it entranced the boys, that mobile gave me free time! When Sally was born, the mobile didn't cast the same spell over her. Then, I was disappointed. Now, I understand. Our daughter, like most females, found people more interesting than gadgets.

Fourth-grade teacher Carrie Danforth says that when she asks the boys what they did all weekend, she is likely to get a list of activities. When she asks the girls, they will talk about sleepovers, putting polish on each other's nails, and what they talked about.[27]

I asked our seven-year-old grandson, Simeon, if he liked playing with his friend Hunter or his friend Travis better. He said, "The same."

His nine-year-old sister, Jessa, piped up, "For girls it matters who we are with—*for boys* it just matters what they have. Simeon likes Hunter and Travis the same because they have the same stuff: Play Station and Star Wars."

Not offended at all by his sister's comment, Simeon nodded in agreement. I smiled.

My friend Jean said, "When my husband goes out to play golf, I'll ask him, 'Who are you golfing with today?' He'll answer, 'Anyone I can hook up with!' I would never golf that way. I want to choose my companion!"

Women's Intuition

The right brain is also the intuitive hemisphere. Dr. Donald Joy compared a woman's mind to a giant computer: She spits out the right answer, but there's no way to check her logic, and even she can't tell you how she got it.[28] Our accuracy in first impressions tends to be higher than those of men. Dr. Dobson says that when he and his wife, Shirley, come home after meeting with people for the first time, Shirley will have correctly assessed personality and character. Dobson says, "Here I've got a Ph.D. in psychology, but it takes me weeks or months of dealing with the people to come to the same conclusion."[29]

Studies have consistently shown that women are better than men at reading and responding to subtle cues about mood and temperament.[30] Our intuition also gives us speed in perceiving spiritual mysteries. Perhaps that's why God allowed women to be first at the empty tomb. When the women ran to tell the men that Christ had risen, the men "did not believe the women, because their words seemed to them like nonsense" (Luke 24:11). The men had to wait for more facts to satisfy their logical left brains.

Likewise, I believe Mary and Elizabeth intuitively knew the angel was right while their men, Joseph and Zechariah, had to wait for more facts before they could come to the same conclusion. When Gabriel informed Zechariah that his barren wife would be with child, Zechariah, in true left-brain form, responded, "How can I be sure of this?" (Luke 1:18). And Joseph "had in mind to divorce Mary quietly" (Matt. 1:19).

What comfort, therefore, Mary and Elizabeth gave to each other in their greeting scene! Sensitive to each other's need for encouragement, they affirmed each other's faith. Elizabeth lifts Mary's heart as soon as she sees her young cousin by saying, "Good for you, Mary! You believed!"

As we discover the differences in the brain functions between men and women, we appreciate our need for each other. Gary Smalley commented that one of the reasons God said, "It is not good for the man to be alone," (Gen. 2:18) is that the man needs a woman to help him develop the right side of his brain.[31] My husband, Steve, who was blessed with a beautifully strong left brain (he was a whiz at math, surgery, and keeping our lives completely organized) would often tell me I'd strengthened his right brain. "I'm appreciating more and more," he told me once, "the beauty in life: children, puppies, and poetry."

Women Are Natural Nurturers

It makes sense to me that the God who created us with the ability to carry babies under our hearts and nurse them tenderly at our breasts would also equip us with a longing and a skill for responding to the needs of those who are vulnerable.

Most women tend to scatter rose petals on the hard paths of life, whereas men need to be taught to be comforters. When our daughter Sally was little and I left her in Steve's care while I was out of town, she had a complaint to voice upon my return. She snuggled next to me on the sofa and confided intently:

> Daddy doesn't know how to wake me up. He doesn't turn on the music or give me a back rub or even kiss me good morning. He just flicks on the big light and says, "Time to get up!" That's not a very good morning greeting. Will you tell him, for next time?

(I did. He repented.)

Once I stood on our covered porch while mothball-sized hail pelted the ground. It also relentlessly pelted a mother robin who sat stoically on her nest in a nearby plum tree, protecting her scrawny, newly hatched babies from the onslaught. Her instinct was so strong that I found myself thinking of Dr. Seuss's Horton, the elephant who subbed for a lazy Mayzie bird while she flew off to Palm Beach:

> So Horton kept sitting there, day after day. And soon it was Autumn. The leaves blew away. And then came the Winter ... the snow and the sleet! And icicles hung from his trunk and his feet. But Horton kept sitting, and said with a sneeze, I'll stay on this egg and I won't let it freeze.[32]

("Aha!" say those of you who feel I have been guilty of stereotyping men and women. "Horton was a male elephant!" It's true, but Horton was a most exceptional male.)

Our Culture Discourages Male Friendliness

On the fertile field of a woman's innate friendliness rolls the snowball of culture. Father robin has no fear that carrying dangling earthworms to his young will tarnish his masculine reputation, but the human male is plagued by such fears.

While little girls are playing with dolls, practicing nurturing, little boys are on teams—competing. Elliot Engel commented that the male twosome seems to be designed "more for combat than for comfort." Whether it's the tennis court or the law court, men are expected to compete. "This almost ensures," Elliot observes, "that our relationship will never develop into intimacy but will stay at a superficial guarded level. Vulnerability is not accepted as a healthy component of male relationships."[33]

Culture augments heredity in the areas of smiling and praise. Studies show that even in infancy, girls smile more than boys.[34] As we grow older, we find that it's considered feminine to smile and masculine to be stern and impassive. As Brownies we sang about "the great big Brownie smile," but I doubt that our male counterparts were singing about "the great big Cub Scout smile."

Author Marian Sandmaier pointed out that our world is full of smiling role models for little girls to follow—"from Miss America to Marie Osmond"—and of glowering role models for little boys, "from the lonesome cowboy to the slouching rock star."[35]

After I told my husband that research shows women smile and praise more than men, he had a humorous interaction with a male patient and his family. Steve characterized Mike as the "strong, silent type," sparing with his compliments and smiles. Steve's surgery gave Mike relief after suffering for years with back pain. It was Mike's wife, however, who caught up with Steve in the hospital corridor to thank him. Smiling warmly, she said, "Doctor, Mike just can't believe his pain is finally gone. He's very grateful, but he's just not the kind who could ever tell you to your face. So I wanted to do it for him."

Later, during Steve's gentle examination, Mike scowled while his wife and mother looked on. Knowing better than to take Mike's countenance personally, Steve couldn't resist teasing his patient with a parting remark. As he turned to walk out the door, Steve said, "Mike, my wife is writing a book on the friendships of women. She has found that all through their lives, women smile more than men." The women burst into gales of laughter and the tiniest flicker of a smile crossed Mike's face.

There are those who are telling us that if we want to succeed in the career world we had better wipe those smiles from our faces. Severity, it seems, increases clout. Frankly, I think it would be better if we could influence men to be friendlier rather than becoming less so ourselves. "A cheerful heart is good medicine," Solomon tells us, "but a crushed spirit dries up the bones" (Prov. 17:22).

Kind words and smiles definitely brighten the world. A woman friend catches my eye in church and smiles—and I feel cared for, lifted.

Our bond has been recognized and affirmed. When I speak, it is usually women who are smiling at me, nodding their support, encouraging me, and appeasing my fears. I receive notes of encouragement almost every week from women friends, but my husband rarely received one from another man. The patients who did write to thank him were almost invariably women.

Surly cowboys and hard-boiled detectives are fine for television, but I am not drawn to them as friends. I stay away from them just as I stay away from a cat with an arched back. People—men and women—who have contagious laughs, words of encouragement, and warm and caring smiles are the ones who find themselves magnetically drawing others. I am drawn to them just as I am drawn to a dog whose tail thumps when he sees me.

Women See Themselves in a Web of Relationships

Carol Gilligan, associate professor of education at Harvard University, makes the following insightful observation:

> Since masculinity is defined through separateness while feminin-
> ity is defined through attachment, male gender identity is
> threatened by intimacy, while female gender identity is threatened
> by separation.[36]

Women see themselves as part of a web of relationships. My husband and I noticed that when we asked members of a Sunday school class to introduce themselves with a thumbnail sketch, the women would often mention their relationships with others, whereas the men would simply talk about themselves.

Both men and women want and need affirmation. However, women are more likely to let the affirmer know how much it meant, thereby increasing the cycle. After her first year in women's Bible study, Beth told her group:

> You've changed me. When I first came here, my heart was hard. I
> realize that now. But the way you've reached out to me, the sensi-
> tivity toward God I've seen in your lives, the tears, the embraces ...
> you've made my heart tender. I really didn't think it could happen.
> I feel like I've regained my innocence.

As I read the conversations between Ruth and Naomi, and then, in the New Testament, between Mary and Elizabeth, I see a continual drawing out of one another, an affirming of one another, and a receptivity to one another. Sparks fly back and forth between these women in ever-increasing heat, as iron sharpens iron! (Prov. 27:17). (This is true of David and Jonathan as well, but, as I will show, David and Jonathan were exceptional and, probably, right-brained males.) Consider, for example, the greeting scene between Mary and Elizabeth in Luke's first chapter. Mary has traveled over seventy miles just to be with Elizabeth, and Elizabeth greets her with affirmation after affirmation, letting Mary know clearly that she is "blessed among women." Mary receives this affirmation with joy and praise to God, culminating in one of the most beloved pieces in Scripture: "Mary's Magnificat."

If our relationship with the Lord is strong, then sweet water overflows and the fluidity in our relationships means we can have a lovely effect on each other. Like gently moving streams joining into one river, we round the difficult bends of life together, strengthening each other with a fresh water supply. We are free and flowing and unconcerned with boundaries. This is part of the beauty of the friendships of women, but it is also the danger.

We are afraid to run toward the ocean alone. We feel a sense of panic in solitude. Ironically, it is because we place such a high value on our relationships that we are tempted, sometimes, to be so very cruel.

It is most evident in childhood. Do you remember?

CHAPTER THREE

THE DARKER SIDE OF BEING CRAZY-GLUED

O n a hot, humid August afternoon, Holly and Kate found refuge in the coolness of Holly's basement. Holly's dark braids were flying as Kate rhythmically turned the jump rope, the other end being tied to the doorknob. "Teddy bear, teddy bear, turn around," they chanted. "Teddy bear, teddy bear, touch the ground ..."

The phone rang and Holly's mother appeared at the top of the stairs, interrupting the girls mid-rhyme. "Holly, it's Ramona. She'd like to come over. She could meet Kate. Wouldn't that be fun?"

Holly came halfway up the stairs and looked at her mother warily with dark, foreboding eyes. Then, softly, she whispered, "Mother, you know three just doesn't work with girls."

As a friend of Ramona's mother, Holly's mother hedged. "Honey, jump rope would be better with three. You like Kate and Ramona so much—I think they'd like each other."

Reluctantly, Holly gave in. And Kate and Ramona did like each other. So much so that when Kate got home, she sent Ramona the following letter.

> Dear Ramona,
> How are you? I am fine. Would you like to be best friends? I like you better than I like Holly. I do not like Holly at all any more. Let's not like Holly together.
>
> Your best friend, Kate

The following Friday night, when Holly was spending the night at Ramona's, Ramona brought out the traitorous letter. Ramona's mother was alarmed to hear angry words and wails coming from the girls' room. She opened the door to see the offending letter in shreds on the floor and Holly curled up in a fetal position on the bed, sobbing inconsolably.

I suspect that these girls were not motivated by the desire to hurt but by the desire to secure their own positions. When Holly asked her mother not to allow Ramona to join them in jump rope, she was protecting her relationship with Kate. When Kate wrote Ramona the letter, she was trying to break into the circle. When Ramona revealed Kate's cruel letter, she was trying to show Holly that she was the more worthy friend.

If a girl's needs for intimacy are being met in a friendship or in a close circle of friends, she does not want that threatened by another person. Since the feminine identity is so closely tied to relationships, it is quite natural to want to guard our relationships by making our circle tight—even if the side effect is betrayal.

A male might have trouble empathizing with the girls in the above story. But most of us women understand only too well, for we have experienced this kind of treachery, at least in childhood.

They Drew a Circle and Left Me Out

When Sally was eight, she came home from school one day in tears. She fled up the stairs, slamming her bedroom door behind her. I found her huddled on the floor in the corner, weeping. Hurting like she did, I tried to absorb some of my child's pain by pulling her onto my lap and pressing her head close to my breast. I stroked her hair and waited.

Eventually, between gasps for breath, she sobbed out her story. Her best friends had formed a club and excluded her.

I mentioned the problem to Sally's third-grade teacher at parent-teacher conferences that week. She shook her head in frustration. "These clubs of the girls are a continuing problem. They break each other's hearts. Every year I say, 'no more clubs!' I threaten them. I punish them. But they continue, secretly."

A few days later the club disbanded. The next week a new club formed. I found the evidence when I was emptying my wastebasket. It said:

GIRLS WHO CAN BE IN SALLY'S SECRET CLUB
SALLY
MICHELLE
JILL
STACY

Until little girls can learn to find their security in God alone, exclusive clubs will continue.

Studies show, to our shame, that the feminine sex deserves her reputation for backstabbing. Eva Margolies, in *The Best of Friends, the Worst of Enemies,* observes, "Virtually every research on the subject indicates that while boys can be nasty, they aren't nearly as vicious to one another as girls."[1]

I listened with interest as our daughter and her friend Leisa discussed how quickly the other fifth-grade boys had included a new boy in their recess soccer game. Leisa said, "It's a lot harder to be new if you're a girl. The boys will accept any old boy, but girls are really picky."

A study of first-graders by Dr. Norma Feshback corroborates Leisa's observations. She found that boys are much nicer to a newcomer. The initial response of girls to a new member "was more likely to be one of exclusion and rejection."[2]

A girl's intense desire to be close almost automatically makes her crueler. Newcomers threaten her circle of two. Since boys are more likely to play in groups, one more is welcome. Also, a boy's sense of worth is often tied to his activities—does he excel in math, football, soccer?

While this is not unimportant to a girl, her sense of worth is more apt to be tied to her relationships. Does she have a best friend? Is she one of the popular girls? Girls, more than boys, are threatened by anyone who might change the relationships that give her security and self-esteem. If she needs to turn on another in order to secure her own position, she will.

Adolescence

Elementary school, as challenging as it can be for girls' relationships, can seem like a sparkling blue swimming pool with a friendly lifeguard compared to the crocodile-infested swamp of middle school. Now one must navigate through a maze of classrooms, teachers, and students. The aggression of adolescent girls tends to be hidden, unlike the open physical aggression of boys. A girl knows that paddling her raft through the dark swamp of middle school can be treacherous. Any day a crocodile may lift his threatening jaws from the murky water as she may:

- become suddenly unwelcome at her usual lunch table
- be betrayed by a best friend
- become the target of a bully
- be gossiped about within her own circle
- be the only one *not* invited to a friend's birthday party

Rachel Simmons, in *Odd Girl Out*, says that "at first glance, the stories of girls not being allowed to eat at the lunch table, attend a party, or put their sleeping bag in the middle may seem childish,"[3] but they can leave a girl devastated. Being isolated is very frightening to girls, and we must neither dismiss her feelings nor assume she will be able to work it out by herself. She is struggling in quicksand and desperately longs for someone to care enough to extend a hand.

We have tremendous resources in Christ. God has told us to ask Him for wisdom, and Scripture is full of practical advice. The Word tells us we have not because we ask not, and we need to pray (James 1:5; 4:2).

I remember calling on the Lord for His wisdom when our daughter Sally began seventh grade. Within the first week she was being teased by a group of older girls led by Shannon, who, ironically, went to our church. When Sally walked by Shannon's desk in Spanish class, Shannon stuck out her foot and tripped her. Shannon's friends snickered as Sally picked herself up. Shannon and her friends whispered when Sally walked down the hall. Sally dreaded Spanish class, youth group, and any other place where she might encounter Shannon.

When Sally confided in me, it was tempting to call Shannon's mom, but Sally feared that could backfire. So we prayed about the best way for *Sally* to handle the situation herself. When we prayed, the verse that came into my head was: "Overcome evil with good" (Rom. 12:21). I suggested Sally begin by being nice to Shannon, and to say hi to her when she came into class.

"Mom—how can I?"

"It will be hard—but if Shannon is jealous or mad at you for some reason, Scripture tells us a soft word can turn away wrath. If her motives are evil, Scripture tells us to overcome evil with good. God's Word really has wisdom and power. What have you got to lose?"

Twice Sally said, "Hi," to Shannon, and twice Shannon ignored her.

The next week the church birthday calendar had Shannon's name on it. I suggested Sally give Shannon a card.

"Mom!"

"This is a wonderful opportunity. It's hard to resist someone who keeps being nice to you. I think it is possible that Shannon didn't mean for this all to escalate—she might have tripped you as a practical joke—but then her friends egged her on, and she was caught. Kindness can break the cycle. A nice birthday card will certainly make her think."

"This is the last time I'm trying. What if they are laughing at me for being nice?"

"I don't think they are. First Peter 3:16 says that your good behavior can make them ashamed. I think you've begun to melt the ice, and this may be the final blast of warm air that will finish the job."

Sally spent a long time at Wal-Mart choosing the right card. She chose a pretty card with tulips on the front that simply said, "Happy Birthday" inside.

Sally came home that night after school bursting with news:

"I walked into Spanish and she was already in her desk. When I walked past her, I put the card on her desk and said, 'Happy Birthday.' She didn't say anything, but I saw her open the card during class.

"After class I smiled at her and said, 'Have a good birthday!' And Mom, she said, 'Thanks.'"

After that, Shannon would smile at Sally and say "Hi." The teasing stopped. When both of the girls were on the high school tennis team two years later, they had a good season together.

Bullies

Abuse is escalating with each generation, for abuse victims become abusers. Bullies are not confined to the male sex. Your daughter may be hesitant to tell you if she is being bullied and may downplay serious trouble until she can "test the waters" and see what kind of action you, as a mother or mentor, might take. If she *is* being bullied, she may fear that you will run to the teacher or to the bully's parents—and that could backfire on her. The only signs you might see are a reluctance to go to school or being generally withdrawn. She'll be more likely to open up to someone who is available and empathetic. If she *does* begin to open up, she'll need reassurance that you will strategize *with* her on how to handle the situation in an effective way. She needs *a godly coach.*

You may feel, "I don't know if I *can* help—some of these situations seem impossible." Rosaline Wiseman, the founder of *Empower,* an organization that helps boys and girls overcome violence, also has step-by-step strategies. Wiseman tells a story of Lori, a new girl to the sixth grade who apparently was a threat to the Queen Bee (Q. B.) of a clique.

A rumor was started by the Queen Bee and her Side-Kick that Lori was a "slut" (even eleven-year-olds may be using that word today). A petition was circulated and signed agreeing that Lori was a slut. Suddenly she had nowhere to sit at lunch, nowhere to feel safe, and no one to talk to at school. Fortunately, when she talked to her mother, her mother took her seriously and Lori really opened up. She helped Lori with Plan A—which was for Lori to confront the Queen Bee directly. Lori's mother was the behind-the-scenes coach and Lori went to school well rehearsed. This is what happened:

> Lori: Can I talk to you for a minute?
>
> Q. B.: What about?
>
> Lori: I know about the petition and it really hurt me. I don't know why something like this would happen, but I want it stopped and I know you have the power to stop it.
>
> Q. B.: Well, too bad, and obviously people agree with me because they signed it too.
>
> Lori: I want it stopped. I don't know why you don't like me so much, but there's nothing I can do about it. I would like us to be civil to each other and respect each other.
>
> Q. B.: Whatever.
>
> Lori: If you ever want to talk to me about why you did this, I would like to hear it. Again, I'm asking you to stop and I really think you have the power to stop it.[4]

What Lori accomplished with her action was to communicate that she wasn't easy prey. She also gave the Queen Bee a reason to stop the rumor—it affirmed her power. If Lori's strategy had not worked, her next step would have been to talk to the teacher. Wiseman has a strategy for that as well as strategies for Plans C and D.

Part of helping young women become competent is to coach them rather than to step in. It is particularly crucial in dealing with bullies. An article in *Psychology Today* stressed, "Bullies don't pick on just anyone." Failing to discuss your discomfort with a bully's actions is "a clear signal that you don't stand up for yourself, and that's her ticket to manipulating and hurting you through dealings with others."[5]

Not only must we coach our daughters to deal with depravity in others, we must help them deal with it in themselves. Mothers attending an in-depth Bible conference in Tennessee were awakened to the depravity in their daughters when *Mean Girls* author Hayley DiMarco came back to the arena to address them after leading a workshop for their fourteen- to nineteen-year-old daughters. When DiMarco asked these girls how many had had a mean girl in their lives, most of their hands went up. When she asked them how many had *been* a mean girl, not only did most of the hands go up, but a cheer went out. Hayley spoke the truth in love to the girls, then spoke to their mothers at the larger conference, and the Lord brought repentance in the girls' conference.

How can we help our daughters to overcome their bent toward cruelty? Telling them to be kind may not be effective because it doesn't deal with the root problem. When girls (and women) are not in a deep love relationship with Jesus, when they do not know what it really means to have Jesus meeting their needs for identity and security, they will continue to be cruel. We must help them truly fall in love with Jesus. How? Pray they will become thirsty for Jesus. Help them behold Him (for to behold Him is to love Him) and model the reality of an exciting love relationship with Jesus to them. When the vertical relationship with Jesus is wonderful, then horizontal relationships with others become lovely as well.

Jill, who raised three godly daughters, said, "I often told my girls that there would definitely be times when they would have to stand alone. Sometimes your unwillingness to go along with a behavior you know isn't pleasing to God will exclude you from a group of girls. I told them, you may have to stand alone, but stand tall. Jesus is pleased with you."

If you are a mother, teacher, or authority figure, you *can* do things to reduce bullying. It is your responsibility to make your home, classroom, team, or carpool a safe place emotionally as well as physically. You need to get involved, discipline, and also find ways to minister to the bully, who has his or her own deep hurts. People who are hurt are people who hurt people—but Christ can help us overcome evil with good.

College Sororities

The world of college sororities is simply a continuation of the cruelty of adolescence. Their main disgrace is in the way they choose who will become a member. The more prestigious the sorority, the greater their power to exclude. To my shame, I fully participated in this system as a young woman at Northwestern University (N.U.). My only defenses are that I was immature and had not yet trusted Christ as my Lord.

My roommate my freshman year was Heather. Someone had matched us up and assigned us to the only room with a private bath because they liked our names. (My given name is Meredith.) To our mutual joy, we liked each other immensely and became best friends. Heather, a quiet violin major, was more mature than I, and not enamored with sororities. She tried to point out the value of making friends cautiously (Proverbs 12:26 warns, "a righteous man is cautious in friendship") and the danger of throwing in our lot for four years with one group based on a few days of parties. But so strong was my need for connection, so fearful was I of not being identified with a sorority, that I convinced Heather to go through rush and pledge with me.

We chose the sorority I liked best and voted together. Heather's was a "suicide" vote—that is, she requested only that one vote, and if she didn't get in on that vote then she was out of the sorority. She would then be forced to join the "independents"—a group that at that time made up only 7 percent of the population at N.U. and was, of course, snubbed by the sorority women. The sorority voted to accept me and reject my best friend. I was shocked by our forced separation, for I would eventually have to live apart from Heather in the sorority house.

In my naïveté I expected we would both get in: I, because I wanted it so much, and Heather, because she was a lovely brunette with enormous dark eyes, and I knew that beauty was the top requirement. But Heather had told them that she was unsure whether she was going to pledge, and so they coldly decided to reject her before she rejected them.

As a sophomore, I saw the ugly insides of rush. Amidst punch and hors d'oeuvres, we were to chat amiably with the freshmen as they came through the house. After a few minutes of conversation, we were to make mental note of which girls met our high standards. In my sorority, the less attractive members (the ones who were dubbed "surprises" on pledge day) were kept busy in the kitchen. (Can you imagine what being kept behind closed doors would do to your self-esteem?)

I wish I had followed the commendable example of my two older sisters, who had the integrity to deactivate after getting a close look at rush, but my intense need for a feeling of belonging to my feminine friends was stronger than my desire to choose the higher, kinder road.

At night during rush, the cruelty intensified. We discussed the merits and defects of each girl. We knew we had the power to break hearts, and break hearts we did. By keeping a girl out, we were affirming to each other how special and how tight our circle was. I was a part of this evil, and along with the shame, took some delight in securing my position as one of the special ones.

C. S. Lewis says that just as we find joy in discovering a friend who loves the same beauty—the same poet, truth, or music—so do we delight in sharing a secret evil: "Even now, at whatever age, we all know the perilous charm of a shared hatred or grievance. (It is difficult not to hail as a friend the only other man in college who really sees the faults of the Sub-Warden.)"[6]

When I was a student at Northwestern University, the school was 93 percent Greek. Today the campus is less than 50 percent Greek and there are also thriving Christian groups as healthy alternatives. If your daughter is going to a secular school, encourage her to consider a Christian group instead of a sorority. (You can find out if they exist on a particular campus through the Web sites for Navigators, InterVarsity, and Campus Crusade.) In a day of feminism you might think a system that judges women primarily on their outward appearance would be a dying system—but it is alive and well, and its shameful secrets are fiercely guarded.

Alexandra Robbins, a former staff member of the *New York Times,* tried to get information about sororities and finally had to go under-cover as a sorority girl to get the true picture of the Greek world. Her book, *Pledged,* reveals rampant negative behavior: drugs, psychological abuse, extreme promiscuity, racism, and eating disorders. When asked if she would allow her daughter to be part of a sorority, Robbins said:

> The national offices are so concerned with things like money and image that they've lost touch with the girls as individuals. I think if they wiped out the idea of pledging, didn't force girls to live in a house together, and really overhauled the rush process then I'd be much more likely to happily let a girl in. Some parents take sororities so seriously that they hire rush consultants, which are kind of like pageant consultants to guide their girls through rush.[7]

Many sorority women will tell you that their experience was a good one, and I am sure that can be true. I also know that alumni can be fiercely defensive, for I have certainly experienced their fury. When I gave one girl's testimony from a well-known women's college in the original *Friendships of Women,* and mentioned the school by name, I was amazed at how many angry letters and phone calls I received. I knew this young woman well, knew her to be a woman of integrity, yet her simple statement of being very hurt and of having her values torn apart by the rush system drew fire such as I have seldom experienced as a writer.

At worst, sororities can be cults with fierce allegiance by their members. My own initiation involved donning a white robe, making secret pacts, and participating in a mysterious ceremony. Even though I didn't know the Lord at that time, it still felt wrong. Yet, my need to belong was so intense, I went along with it.

At best, sororities tend to emphasize outward appearance over inward character. When you decide who will belong and who won't in a matter of ten minutes, how can you judge anything *except* outward appearance? When I was on the Focus on the Family radio program the first time with *Friendships of Women,* Dr. Dobson courageously called sororities "a flesh market."

It saddens me that so many colleges still introduce freshmen to their world with the cruelty of rush. The nature of sororities seems to bring out the worst in women, for we want so much to be securely connected to others.[8]

Though we do become kinder in maturity, and certainly in Christ, we still are prone to inflict wounds on others.

Gossip

There are two words for gossip in the Old Testament Scriptures. The first is the Hebrew word *rakiyl,* which means "traveling with confidences." Betrayal is involved, for you are sharing a secret that should have remained in your own heart.

Since women are willing to make themselves vulnerable to one another, they have more to spill. One pastor told me, "It's good that women are willing to reveal more of themselves to each other, for without that, you don't have intimacy. But women often fail to be trustworthy with those revelations." Why are we tempted to be faithless? Because of our strong desire for connection.

When a woman whispers, "Don't tell anyone else, but ..." there is a feeling that she trusts you, you are a privileged one, and you are enjoying the spark of intimacy and some juicy news. Even prayer requests can be a spiritual cover for "traveling with confidences" that were supposed to remain with you.

One woman remarked that she was fairly careful not to break

confidences when talking to another woman, but that she felt free to share those same confidences with her husband. "Even though I know that telling him may influence him negatively against that person, I can't seem to help myself. I need to unload to someone, and I think we have that right in marriage."

"Hey, wait a minute," a single woman responded. "It sounds fine to say, 'I would only tell my husband,' but where does that leave me? Don't single people need to unload too?"

When I'm going through pain in my life inflicted on me by someone, I have felt a need to talk it over with my husband or another trusted friend. I have wrestled with this. Is this gossip? The other Hebrew word translated *gossip* has a darker connotation than "traveling." It is *nirgan* and comes from a Hebrew root word meaning "to roll to pieces."

If my sharing is going to roll someone to pieces, then I *am* gossiping. I believe if we examine our hearts and are confident that our motive is to gain wisdom for the situation and not to roll the person to pieces, then there may be some justification in going to a closemouthed spiritual giant. But a higher road would be to wait and see if time will bring healing. I must guard against revenge and my intense desire to verify that I am in the inner circle.

One woman understood her own behavior when she said, "I have this desire to confirm in my confidant's mind that she should think more of me than so-and-so, who's been unfair to me."

Karen, a college chemistry teacher, told me that she likes being the only woman in an otherwise all-male department because there's a minimum of infighting and gossip. Her husband's music department is beleaguered by a few gossiping women. Although men do gossip, women gossip more. Until we can learn to find our security in God alone, we will gossip.

Women's Bible Studies

Most women's Bible study groups form beautiful bonds within weeks. Women are sharing vulnerably, weeping, laughing, and encouraging one another, evidencing their gift for intimacy. Each rejoices in the comfortable, womblike warmth of the group.

It takes tremendous maturity to venture outside in order to befriend and invite others in. When your own needs for intimacy are being met, it's easy to slide into complacency about the needs of others.

If a newcomer does come, she senses the group's intimacy and feels like an outsider looking in. The invitations to lunch, the phone calls, and the notes aren't nearly as common as they should be. Too often, the newcomer doesn't come back.

Christian women are also hesitant to divide a Bible study group as their numbers grow. This is a subtle modification of the cruelty of elementary clubs and college sororities. Until women learn to find their security in God alone, Bible studies will be tainted with exclusiveness.

Helping Each Other Find Strength in God

The difference between secular and Christian friendships is enormous, *if* we are availing ourselves of the wonderful resources in Christ. You will see a pattern in the three biblical friendships we will study (we'll start with Naomi and Ruth in the next chapter). Instead of finding strength in each other, they helped each other find strength in God.

One Minnesota woman's church had the women who were doing a Bible study on hospitality hold one another accountable for *not* being exclusive. Instead of talking to their closest friends and family during the social break between church and Sunday school, they determined to talk to visitors, children, or people they didn't know well. Jesus stressed the importance of *not* just being hospitable to our friends, family, and "rich neighbors" for they will "repay" you, but to reach out to those who may *not* repay you, and "you will be repaid at the resurrection of the righteous" (Luke 14:14).

Each week the women would begin their study by sharing whom they had talked to at the break, and during the prayer time they would pray for those people and also for courage and wisdom in obeying again the next Sunday. One woman reflected: "It was frightening for me because I am such a shrinking violet. I *had* to lean on the Lord—asking Him for wisdom on who to talk to, and asking Him to let His love flow through me. And you know what? He really answered! I *know* I helped some visitors feel welcomed, made friends with some children, and overall, sensed God's pleasure. Now the break, instead of being this dreaded weekly time, is my little weekly adventure."

Christ can completely change our approach to friendships. Author

Win Couchman told me once, "Sometimes when I first meet an interesting woman I have a lust to acquire her as a friend—like a possession. But if I pray—God may completely change my attitude, and my motive becomes purer, or, I find myself drawn to another woman!"

As we grow in Him, as we help each other find strength in Him, we will be protected from the sin that women are most prone to in their friendships: relational idolatry. I've received more mail about the next chapter than any in the whole book, and I pray it will minister to you.

Chapter Four

RELATIONAL IDOLATRY

It was a cyclical pattern for me to cling too tightly to my girlfriends.
For example, I knew Brooke's schedule well, so, during her break, if I didn't
hear my computer say, "You've got mail!" I'd become anxious.

— CHRISTY

S ometimes friends are a surprise gift from God. Rachel, an energetic and witty young woman, has been that for me. I was drawn to her initially because of her lifestyle of radical obedience. She and her husband, though newlyweds, were regularly practicing biblical hospitality. They had befriended their neighbors and now had a neighborhood beginner's Bible study. They had invited a mentally retarded adult to live with them. And they were always the ones who would invite newcomers home with them for Sunday dinner.

I was curious as to how a twenty-five-year-old who did not grow up in a Christian home became so mature—so I invited Rachel out for lunch. As so often happens with the Lord, when you put your hand in His and let Him lead you in friendship, He has more for you than you ever could have imagined. Such was the case with Rachel. I had no idea that she had been set free of the practice of homosexuality and that she would make such a vital contribution to my writing of *The Friendships of Women*.

Rachel's story opened my eyes. Not only did she help me understand how someone could be tempted by homosexuality, but she also helped me recognize the astonishing truth that the root problem of lesbians is similar to a problem most women struggle with: relational idolatry. This is the worship of people or, put another way, dependency on a human relationship rather than on God.

Rachel

As we headed toward my favorite restaurant, a cozy place with booths, candles, and the smell of homemade soup, Rachel casually asked me what I was writing presently. When I told her it was a book on the friendships of women, she gasped. I looked at her curiously.

At first, she dodged. "There's a need for that book, and I would definitely read it."

I wasn't satisfied. I knew, intuitively, that there was more behind her startled reaction. Beseechingly, my eyes met hers. After a minute she responded. "Just give me a little time to gather my courage and I'll tell you." She took a deep breath. "I think the Lord must have arranged for us to have this time together, so I'll tell you," she promised. "I will."

Rachel was *so* nervous—I really couldn't imagine what she was going to tell me. We waited until we'd both ordered, and then Rachel took the plunge:

"I was in a lesbian relationship in college."

I could tell Rachel was watching me to see how I'd respond. I know, from another friend who has been delivered from these chains, that she is *very* careful whom she tells, for the church's record is mighty poor in showing compassion to those who have struggled or are struggling with *this* sin. I grabbed her hands and thanked her for trusting me so quickly. Her eyes filled with tears and she said:

"I have to be true to a vow I made to God. When I was in those terrible chains, I promised Him, 'Set me free and I'll help other women in homosexual bondage.' When you told me the title of your book, I knew that, to be obedient, I needed to tell you my story. He has set me free and this may be a chance to help others."

I pulled out my notebook and Rachel began to tell me her story. While not attempting to justify herself, she tried to help me understand why so many women fall into this trap.

"I don't know how it happened," Rachel began, speaking softly and hesitatingly. "I do know that I had a deep need for affirmation. And homosexual relationships between women," she paused, trying to gauge my reaction, "are different in character from homosexual relationships between men. In my opinion, men have such strong physical urges that the priority is often sexual. But with women, there is a nurturing tenderness which can seem deceptively beautiful."

Before I tell Rachel's story, I think it would be helpful to look at a few key insights Christian counselors have gained about homosexuality.

Christian Counselors on Homosexuality

Counselors have identified several situations that can make a woman more vulnerable to the temptation of homosexuality. Rachel's vulnerability to this sin was increased by childhood sexual abuse. A girl who is abused by a man is understandably going to be repulsed by men sexually. She may feel much safer with a woman. Because of the deterioration of the family and the easy access to child pornography on the Internet, sexual abuse is rampant. When one of my daughters was in grade school, she brought a new friend home after school. My first warning sign was that when I asked this little girl to check with her mother to see if she could play, she said she didn't need to. Then, when I took her home, I decided to walk her to the door, hoping to meet her mother. When she opened the door, she called out, "Mom? Rodney?"

"Who's Rodney?" I asked.

"My mom's boyfriend."

"When will someone be home?"

"I don't know. It's okay. I'm alone a lot."

I saw that there were beer cans, cigarette butts, and porn littering the floor. What easy prey she would be. It was really a wake-up call to me, and I realized this kind of living situation is happening to girls all over our country. As live-in lovers and porn increases, so does childhood sexual abuse. Women who have been sexually abused as children often have a propensity to avoid men and to be drawn to other women.

Dr. Jane Flax believes the most common factor making a woman vulnerable to lesbianism is growing up with a cold, indifferent mother.[1] (Don't hesitate to express affection to your daughter, or she may one day try to fill that need through a lesbian relationship.) A passive father and a dominating mother is another lethal combination—for the daughter neither respects men nor has a positive role model in a woman. How many women belittle their husbands! So many women have never learned to show their husbands honor, speaking the truth in love instead of belittling them with insults.

The power of the gay agenda should not be underestimated. Gays have produced curricula, movies, and television programs to promote their agenda. Those who say the practice of homosexuality is sinful or harmful are portrayed as close-minded fundamentalists and hateful bigots.

Children and teens are asked to consider and even experiment to see if they might be gay. There is a period in adolescence when girls and boys naturally feel some attraction for both sexes. Many young people who never would have considered experimenting with a same-sex relationship in the past are doing so today. They may find that initial experience enjoyable, much in the same way that masturbation is enjoyable, and they then decide they must have been born a homosexual.

The Bible says the practice of homosexuality is sin (see Lev. 18:22; 20:13; Rom. 1:26–27; 1 Cor. 6:9). There are so-called gay churches who, blinded by sin, are attempting to distort the Scriptures and deny their clarity. They say, for example, that the sin of Sodom was not homosexuality but inhospitality (see Gen. 19:1–5), and deliberately ignore the fact that Jude 7 clarifies the fact that Sodom's sin was sexual perversion.[2]

I have had women come up to me after I have spoken on the friendships of women at retreats and tell me that they do not see a conflict between their practice of lesbianism and Christianity. Satan is a master deceiver. The three lies he tells most frequently to those caught in this lifestyle are: "You are not really sinning"; "You can never change"; and, "You will not be happy if you leave this lifestyle."

Does that mean that no one is born with a tendency toward homosexuality? Not necessarily. The jury is still out on that point, but it could be that just as some have a genetic tendency toward alcoholism or violence, some have a genetic tendency toward homosexuality. That does not mean, however, that these tendencies cannot be overcome, for God doesn't give us commands that are impossible to obey. It is more difficult, for example, for a person with a predisposition toward alcoholism not to fall into that bondage, but neither does he or she *have* to be an alcoholic. We would direct such a person to a twelve-step program and know that he or she could be set free.

As a matter of fact, our predisposition toward sin is embedded deep within *all* of us. I was born with a propensity to greed, to lying, to self-ishness, and to all kinds of sin. I lied before I could walk, I stole nickels from my mother's purse when I was a first-grader, and my favorite topic of conversation was (and often still is) myself.

I can't imagine anyone accepting this statement from me: "This is the way I was born. I must be true to who I really am. Don't ask me to deny my nature. I am a liar, a thief, and I must be focused continually on myself. Accept me as I am!" Instead, I know that denying myself is my only hope. I die daily so that the Holy Spirit can flourish in me. I don't have to be in bondage to sin.

Writer for *World* magazine Andrew Seu writes that "sin runs deeper than we thought. Like the mildewed cloth that the Mosaic law threw on the pyre, 'What a wretched man I am!' Paul exclaims upon discovering this (Rom. 7:24–25). 'Who will deliver me from this body of death? Thanks be to God through Jesus Christ our Lord.'"[3] God abundantly supplies the resources we need to abstain from sin, even sin that is embedded in us from the womb. Rachel and Laura's story gives us hope.

It Began As a Beautiful Friendship

Many male homosexuals are masculine and many female homosexuals are feminine. Often individuals will not take on characteristics of the opposite sex in dress, conversation, or interests until they have chosen a homosexual lifestyle.

Rachel and Laura don't fit the physical stereotype often given to les-bians. Though Rachel is lanky and comfortable in jeans, her gentle manner, blond curls, and porcelain complexion give her a cameo look. Laura is diminutive, dark, and shapely. Her hair cascades down her back in gentle waves. If she were to walk past a city construction site, she would draw wolf whistles.

A traumatic childhood can increase vulnerability to homosexual-ity. Maxine Hancock and Karen Mains cite a study in their excellent book *Child Sexual Abuse* showing a possible link between childhood abuse and lesbianism.[4] In this study, conducted by Karen Meiselman, seven of twenty-three daughters who had experienced incest had "become gay or had significant experiences or conflicts centered on homosexual feelings."[5]

Rachel had been abused sexually, repeatedly and traumatically, by an uncle when she was a child. She said, "He made me do things I wouldn't consider doing in my marriage." It was difficult, therefore, as a young woman, for Rachel to feel an attraction for men. But both Rachel and Laura are convinced that what happened to them could happen to anyone who doesn't have God in first place as the central focus of her life. Rachel told me how her friendship with Laura began:

> It was completely innocent at first. We had that immediate rapport that I believe is a gift from God. Laura is one of the most sensitive people I've ever met. Tenderhearted, she cares deeply about the hurts of others. The unfortunate side effect of that characteristic is that she's easily bruised. She fed off my strength, my ability to roll with the punches. I fed off her sensitivity. We were a great match. And there was something about Laura that intrigued me, something that made me want to know her better.

"When did the problem begin?" I asked Rachel. "And why?"

The Slippery Slide from Soul Mates to Dependency

> I had a void in my life. I didn't understand that that void was created in me to be filled with God, so I turned to Laura. We began to spend too much time together—taking walks, drinking and partying together, talking into the wee hours of the morning. We began to rely on each other for everything. I see now that's when Satan got a foothold. Everything became a blur as we focused completely on each other: college, our studies, our goals for graduation, fellow students—none of that was important. All that mattered was each other.... My love for Laura kept growing. I was shocked to find myself longing to hold her. Just put my arms around her. But I didn't.

In Romans 1:21–25, we are told that the first step leading to homosexuality is worshipping the created thing rather than the Creator. We are wading into quicksand when we begin to look to another person for what God should be in our lives.

In a helpful booklet, *Emotional Dependency: A Threat to Close Friendships,* Lori Thorkelson Rentzel says, "Whether or not physical involvement exists, sin enters the picture when a friendship becomes a dependent relationship."[6] In a healthy friendship, we desire to see our friend reach her potential—it is a giving friendship in which we build her up, encourage her to reach out to others, and find ways to serve God.

Though most of us may not feel tempted by homosexuality, I believe the evidence is strong that we are tempted by dependency. An emotionally dependent relationship produces bondage. If you have a best friend, do any of your feelings for her sound like the warning signs Thorkelson describes?

- you experience frequent jealousy, possessiveness, and a desire for exclusivism, viewing other people as a threat to the relationship
- you prefer to spend time alone with this friend and become frustrated when this does not happen
- you become irrationally angry or depressed when this friend withdraws slightly[7]

These signs were present in Rachel and Laura's friendship. The scene was set for a lesbian relationship. Rachel said:

> I'll never forget the night. We'd been drinking, playing cards, feeling loose. At one point I looked up at Laura and we exchanged a penetrating look that ripped my heart. I felt the beauty of love and the pain of passion. I knew what was going to happen.

Rachel told me that after the first night she was physically intimate with Laura, she felt "so ashamed."

> It was hard to face Laura the next day when we were both sober. We both apologized to the other and attributed it to being drunk out of our gourds. I wanted to believe it would never happen again, but on the other hand, I wanted it to.

So did Laura. John White writes, "Once I experience physical pleasure with a member of my own sex, I am more likely to want to experience it again. The more frequently I experience it, the more fixed the pattern will become."[8]

White also observes that liquor is a fairly common denominator in female homosexuality.[9] Because neither Rachel nor Laura could face the stark reality of what they were doing, they used liquor as an excuse. They would party, drink, and become physically intimate.

> Finally, however, we didn't need liquor to become intimate. The amazing thing is, I didn't believe we were practicing homosexuality. That, I knew instinctively, would be wrong. "How," I asked myself, "could anything this beautiful be wrong?" Orgasm was not the goal—I never experienced it or wanted to. Without it, our expression of love seemed purer, less selfish. "We aren't homosexuals," I told myself again and again. "We're just very special friends expressing our love."

Rachel's feelings soared from great happiness to soul-wrenching misery. "It wasn't just the fear of being discovered, but the innate knowledge that despite my rationalization, what we were doing was very, very wrong."

I find it interesting that Rachel knew in her heart that her behavior was wrong. She hadn't been taught that because she had grown up in a liberal church that didn't use the Bible frequently, and she was taught that our God is a loving God who would never condemn anyone for anything. But God's Spirit was nudging Rachel, whispering danger.

There's a solemn warning in the first chapter of Romans to those who are practicing homosexuality and ignoring the still, small voice of the Holy Spirit. In time, God gives them over to a depraved mind so that they actually become confused over what is right and what is wrong (Rom. 1:24–28). Rachel, as she has testified, was beginning to feel some of that confusion, but before God gave her over to a depraved mind, He shouted the truth to Laura.

> We'd been drinking heavily one night when suddenly Laura broke down, sobbing uncontrollably. She completely floored me by telling me that our relationship was going to result in eternal suffering in hell. I didn't know what to say. I was stunned.

What Laura had never told Rachel was that as a junior-high student at a youth retreat, she had committed her life to Christ. Rachel believes that it was the light of Christ burning in Laura, however dimly, that first attracted her to Laura.

> She was so compassionate and caring. But I didn't know why. I had seen her with her Bible, and I thought it was kind of neat. But she hadn't talked to me about spiritual truths—until that night. Then she poured out her testimony and showed me the Scriptures.

A Kaleidoscope of Emotions

> A kaleidoscope of emotions poured through me—the intense fear of losing Laura, the shame of sin, and the hope of deliverance. I knew she was serious about changing when she told me she had booked a flight to Sarasota over spring break. A strong Christian couple down there had offered to help her. She hoped, she told me weeping, "they will help me straighten out my life, because I can't do it myself."

Laura went to Sarasota. Most Christian counselors would agree that she took the first two necessary steps for breaking her chains. She admitted that her homosexual lifestyle was sinful, and she sought counseling from mature Christians.

In God's uncanny timing, Rachel had planned to spend her spring break at a journalism seminar in nearby Tampa. When Laura's Christian friends realized Rachel was so close, they invited her down for counsel as well. During that time, Rachel and Laura surrendered their lives fully to Christ: Rachel for the first time, and Laura in recommitment. Rachel said,

> The day that I dropped to my knees, I promised Jesus that if He would deliver me from the mess I was in, I would turn around and glorify Him. Someday, I vowed, I would help others who were in the same bondage.

The road to healing for Rachel and Laura was not without pain. They were not instantly delivered from their desire for each other. They stumbled and fell a few times, but there was no joy in the sin anymore.

Deliverance

Counselors advised a time of separation, and they obeyed. Laura moved to another part of the country. Despite the initial pain of obedience, both longed for full deliverance. They longed for normal lives with husbands and children. During that time they kept in touch by letter and phone. Reflecting on those two years of physical separation, Rachel said:

> There were times when I didn't think I'd get over Laura. There were times I thought I might fall into it with someone else. But, slowly, as I chose to obey, I knew God was doing a work in my heart. In time, the overwhelming feelings I had for Laura, I learned to have in an uplifting way for Christ.

Both Rachel and Laura are now happily married, serving the Lord, and good friends. Rachel is keeping her promise and working with other women who are in the bondage of lesbianism. She said:

> If they've lived in this lifestyle a long time, their chains are tight. They also have to deal with tremendous pressure from their partner and from the gay community not to change. That's why a move can be so helpful. I want to give these women hope. Christ can break chains if you are determined to obey. I now know that our friendship became unbalanced when we began to look to each other for the fulfillment of our lives. Every day, I need to choose to keep Christ as the first and foremost focus of my life. I believe any relationship, even that between a husband and a wife, is in the danger zone when they look to each other for the completion they should have in Christ.

In her book, *The Long Road To Love,* Darleen Bogle tells of spending seventeen years in the gay culture before deliverance.[10] As she hardened her heart to the Spirit's prompting, she fell into other kinds of sin: occult practices, stealing, and even murder. Her deliverance included deliverance from demon possession.

It is a frightening thing to turn your back on God. It is important to respond to His first prompting and not to harden your heart. So though you may not identify with homosexuality, if you see in yourself a tendency to lean on another person for your fulfillment in life rather than God, recognize this as sin and turn from it. (There are some wonderful resources available, including a great, free online Bible study. I've listed this information in the notes.)[11]

It is also vital to realize that you don't have to be in a homosexual lifestyle to be caught in the bondage of relational idolatry.

Relational Idolatry

Christy is a very capable professional woman who has had a personal relationship with the Lord from a young age. Yet, like many Christian women, her friendships were not healthy. Christy told me:

> It was a cyclical pattern for me to cling too tightly to my girlfriends. For example, the friendship I was in when I finally began to realize my problem was with Brooke. We communicated a lot through e-mail and she would e-mail me during her breaks at work. I knew her schedule well, so if I didn't hear my computer

say, "You've got mail!" I'd become anxious. I'd wonder, "Have I done something wrong?" I'd e-mail her—and I wouldn't quit until I received a response.

My anxiety would heighten when a third party, like a boyfriend, would come into the picture. I felt like our relationship was threatened, and it would affect me physically. I actually felt like I had the flu—my stomach was so frequently upset.

Because Christy was involved in the body of Christ, she had healthy friends who became concerned about her. Christy said, "I remember when Kathy Troccoli said that *she couldn't see she was sick when she was bulimic*—but her friend Allyson made her strip off all her clothes and stand in front of the mirror, telling her she *had* to get help. In a sense, that's what my healthy friends did for me. My friends said to me, 'This is a pattern in you. Your response to these friends isn't healthy. You need help. Please see a counselor.'" Christy did, and explains:

> It was through my counselor that I first became aware of the term "relational idolatry." As soon as she said the phrase, I knew it was a correct diagnosis, suddenly helping me understand that I was sinning against God. I was worshipping a person. I remember I was doing a Beth Moore study—*Breaking Free*—and studying about the kings that wouldn't take down the high places. They worshipped idols. I thought, *That's me!* I wrote Brooke and told her, "I can't explain it now, but I am realizing I need help. I can't e-mail or talk to you while I am getting counseling."
>
> She tried to understand, but it was difficult for her. Eventually I was able to explain and she not only understood, but was thankful. Today our friendship is healthy and restored. I just helped Brooke put together a slide show for her wedding reception. We had a great time talking about her upcoming marriage and plans for me to visit them.
>
> After I was in counseling for six months, I spent another eighteen months doing a lot of reading and Bible study on the subject of codependency. I truly am free. My friendships are healthy and restored. I have a joy, peace, and a much deeper relationship with the Lord. He came and filled the void that I was using people to try to fill.

Best Friend Versus a Network of Friends

"For me," Christy said, laughing, "*best* is a four-letter word. It's dangerous for me to have someone whom I consider my best friend."

As I write, I have a group of women at my cabin in Wisconsin. Christy is one of them, as well as her good (not best!) friend Ellen, a woman who has been a missionary in Romania and is now on staff at her church in the States. Ellen has also experienced the bondage of relational idolatry.

Ellen was led to the Lord by Sandy, a woman a year ahead of her in college. To those on the outside, their friendship appeared beautiful. Ellen was the teachable disciple and Sandy the nurturing mentor. They were always together and much of their time was spent side by side in ministry.

I asked Ellen, "What's wrong with that?" Reflectively, she answered:

> I'd never experienced this kind of care from a woman, and her nurturing was giving me an emotional high. In the same way, Sandy was needy to be needed and was experiencing the same kind of rush. This led to a dependency that was neither healthy nor holy. What looked like a beautiful friendship was, in reality, a selfish one.

By God's grace, Sandy realized the problem. In an act of obedience, she severed the relationship for a time. As they each turned to the Lord, He met the needs of their hearts. "It was a long process," Ellen said, "but for both of us, it was so worth it."

As Ellen, Christy, and I sat on the dock, trailing our bare feet in the water, I asked Ellen: "You and Christy are very close—right?"

They nodded.

"So, explain why your friendship is healthy." Ellen and Christy laughed, squirming a bit with embarrassment at being so exposed and probed. But after a moment, Ellen responded seriously:

> Though I value Christy's friendship and sisterly affection toward me, I am not deceived into thinking it is "life-giving." I remember hearing Larry Crabb in a seminar on "Connecting" in St. Louis. He talked about how in a fallen world we wrongly associate certain things as breeding life or death to our souls. The dynamics of a relationship can feel like a "source of life." Then, when that person withdraws slightly, it feels like death. But

instead, this is bondage. Only Jesus is our source of life. And when a relationship has Him in the middle of it, there is freedom. That's what Christy and I have, and that's why our friendship is healthy.

I've also learned it is much healthier to have a network of friends rather than just one "best friend" upon whom I depend for all my friendship desires.

As I considered this whole issue of feminine dependency, I remember simultaneously observing our then ten-year-old daughter Sally and her friend Tricia. They were practically joined at the hip. They zipped their sleeping bags together, shared their popsicles, and even, when pressed, borrowed each other's underwear and toothbrushes. When they were separated, I sensed Sally's anxiety. They told me they would absolutely die if they didn't get in the same fifth grade.

Pondering their friendship, I asked, "Do you think you are dependent on each other?"

"What does *dependent* mean?" Tricia asked.

Searching quickly for a simple synonym, I said, "Do you think you need each other?"

In unison they chimed, "YES!"

Seeing my perturbed pause, Sally questioned, "Is that bad?"

"Well," I responded, "we should be dependent on Jesus."

"Can't I be dependent on Jesus *and* Tricia?" my daughter asked.

I considered this. (I, who had recently told my extremely capable tax-form-filler-outer, smoke-alarm-putter-upper, sliver-remover husband that if anything happened to him, I hoped a total-care nursing home would accept a forty-two-year-old woman with her three children, contemplated this.) Finally I told Sally, who was waiting expectantly:

> I think we both have some growing up to do. It's important to love our friends, to cherish them, and to be committed to them. Girls and women are good at that—and it's a beautiful side to our friendships. But we need to learn to be dependent, leaning on God, because He's the only one who will never betray us or die or move away.

Sally looked at me quizzically. She could not imagine any of these things happening to destroy her friendship with Tricia.

I, too, never dreamed Steve would die in his fifties and that I would have to live without him. When I hear LeAnn Rimes sing "How can I live without you, how can I breathe without you ..." I so understand. And yet I know that those kinds of thoughts are only rightly directed to Jesus.

God saw my future and knew I would have to live without Steve. So he began to speak the truth gently to me. *Depend on Me, Dee—I am the only One who is the Solid Rock.*

This is a *hard* truth, but God longs for us to understand it. I think that is one of the reasons, among others, that He gave us the book of Ruth.

Let us begin by considering Ruth's mother-in-law, Naomi. Naomi is so much like many of us.

CHAPTER FIVE

CINDERELLA IN THE CHANGE OF LIFE

"Don't call me Naomi," she told them. "Call me Mara,
because the Almighty has made my life very bitter. I went away full,
but the LORD has brought me back empty."

—RUTH 1:20–21

I was six when Disney released Cinderella. My Dad told me: "From the opening scene, you sat straight up in your chair, your little hands gripping the back of the seat in front of you. Not once did you ask for popcorn." I still love Cinderella stories—movies like *Ever After*, *Sleepless in Seattle*, and *The Notebook*—where a truly faithful man rescues a woman in need. In his writings, John Eldredge says men long for the adventure of rescuing someone—and women long for the romance of being rescued.

I was one who was blessed with a truly faithful man. Steve was godly, strong, and oh, so caring. His patients loved him for the time and care he gave them, taking time to pray over each one. Steve prayed, protected, and provided for me. He fought as hard as he could not to die young, to be here for me, his five children, and his patients. But God chose to take Steve home.

I have come to understand that the only One who can *really* rescue me and make all things right is Jesus Christ. He is the only One who will never fail, never forsake me, and never die. One day He *will* appear on a white horse. This scene from Revelation 19:11 puts me in awe:

> I saw heaven standing open, and there before me was a white horse, whose rider is called Faithful and True.

One day He is coming to do battle with my enemies, to sweep me up, and to carry me into a place where I will, indeed, live happily ever after. I will be with Him, be reunited with my loved ones, and have all my tears tenderly wiped away. And in the meantime, He is longing for me to abandon myself to Him, and to trust that He, and He alone, can meet my deepest needs. He wants me to love others—and to cherish my husband, family, and friends—but He warns against trusting in any person, no matter how dear that person may be. That is relational idolatry, putting people before Him. He and He alone is my Solid Rock.

It's easier to see that Rachel was wrong in making another woman her source of joy and security than to look at Naomi and say she was foolish to do the same thing with her husband. For those of us raised on Cinderella, not trusting in your husband, especially if he is a good man, may be a new thought.

Colette Dowling, in her book *The Cinderella Complex*, makes a convincing case for the theory that women are reared for dependency.[1] We are more likely than men to fall into dangerously dependent relationships with either sex. Dowling points out that parents protect their daughters more than their sons, expect their daughters to marry and be cared for, and discourage their daughters more than their sons from taking the kinds of risks that lead to maturity.

Peg, a young woman whose husband left her, felt great anxiety about being thrust into the role of a single mother. She worried about her ability to handle the checkbook, the insurance, the tax forms, and especially about establishing a career. Peg told me:

> Despite what I've been through, I realize that I'm still raising my daughter with the thought that I want her to marry a man who will protect her. I need to shake myself because that may not happen—it may not even be God's will. To be a good mother to Jamie, I need to help her prepare for a career as well as the possibility of marriage and motherhood. I need to teach her that her security is in God and not in a relationship with a man. I hope God does bless her with marriage, but I'm doing her a great injustice if I assume that will be her future.

One of the lessons in the book of Ruth has to do with cherishing the people in our lives, yet not making them our source of security.

Let's open God's family album to the book of Ruth.

Barrenness in Bethlehem

Drought in Scripture is a metaphor for God's judgment, just as rain can symbolize His mercy. How fascinating to study the pictures of the land throughout the book of Ruth, for the story begins with "a famine in the land" that parallels the famine in the hearts of God's people (Ruth 1:1). God had promised *not* to bring a famine to the Promised Land—unless His people were living in disobedience (Deut. 11:11–17).

Elimelech, Naomi's husband, responds to the famine by taking his family to idol-worshipping Moab. He dies as soon as they get to Moab. Many commentators see this as God's judgment. Then the sons follow in their father's unfaithful footsteps. Despite God's clear command for believing men not to marry pagan women, these men marry Moabite women. Pastor John Bronson puts some of the blame on the parents, saying:

> If we watch television shows that repeatedly lift up the values of the world, what do we expect our children to be like? ... If we conduct our lives in the privacy of our own homes without reference to God, what do we expect our children to be like? Who did Elimelech and Naomi expect their sons would marry—the rocks and trees?[2]

Did Naomi try to persuade her boys not to marry Moabite women? Or did she believe that it would be better for them to marry unbelievers than to remain single? Marriage was terribly important to Naomi, as we will continue to see. She herself felt worthless without it—and without the ability, because she had reached menopause, to bear children. She very well may have wanted her sons to marry Moabite women rather than to remain single.

Many Christian women have compromised their values in order to marry because, like Naomi, their security is not based upon their relationship with the Lord but upon marriage. One young woman, engaged to an unbeliever, said, "I know Tom isn't a Christian, but I believe God is blessing us. I think Tom will come to Christ."

Friends tried to warn her that God's Spirit doesn't go contrary to

His Word, but her mind was set. Twenty years later, their home is still divided, their children are divided, and their future looks grim. I know it has been known to work the other way, but it still frightens me to see people fly in the face of God's clear command not to be unequally yoked.

Steve and I tried diligently to impress our children with the importance of marrying believers if they marry. We were pleased to see that point had been staked down when a visitor for dinner asked our then five-year-old son, J. R., what his parents had taught him. Quickly he responded, "I must never marry somebody who doesn't love Jesus, and I must never ride a motorcycle." (Steve spent many hospital nights trying, often in vain, to rescue injured motorcyclists.) We laughed at hearing those two warnings placed side by side, but we actually have been most serious in our hope that J. R. will never endanger his life by doing either of those two things.

I believe Naomi's sons, Mahlon and Kilion, endangered their lives by marrying unbelieving women. The Targum, an ancient commentary written a short time before the Christian era, says that these brothers had their "days cut off because they transgressed the decree of the Lord" in marrying foreign women who worshipped idols.[3] (See Deut. 7:3–4 and Ezra 9:10–14.)

This should sober us if we have a tendency to take God's commands lightly. The meaning of each of the son's names reveals that God knew their destiny: Mahlon means "infirmity" and Kilion means "finished."

Moabites worshipped the god Chemosh. He demanded sexual immorality in the temple. Supposedly when Chemosh saw the people having sexual intercourse, he was inspired to do so as well, and that, somehow (seems strange, I know!) made the land fruitful. Chemosh also asked for the sacrifice of babies on the altar.

Naomi has sometimes been called a female Job. In the first five verses of the book of Ruth she loses her home, her husband, and acquires two barren Moabite daughters-in-law. Finally, Naomi's sons die—and Naomi despairs of God's love for her.

The Emerging Theme of Ruth

If you would take just a few minutes and get out your Bible to mark a few passages in Ruth, an overall theme will emerge and stay in your mind, helping you to see a pattern. I realize some of you may be opposed to writing in your Bibles. Recording artist Kathy Troccoli, who grew up Catholic, remembers the first time she saw someone "write" in the Holy Bible. She thought, *She may be religious—but she's going straight to hell!*

But if you feel free to mark, notice, as I'll show you below, how the book begins with pictures of barrenness: famine, emptiness, and bitterness. Then the tide slowly turns to fruitfulness: fullness, fertility, and joy. As the people trust in themselves and turn from God—there is barrenness. When they begin to turn to Him, the land begins to blossom. Also, as you read, you will come upon Boaz, who is one of the Christ figures hidden in the Old Testament. He provides, protects, and fills empty arms. Here are a few of the pictures:

Barrenness

- There was a famine in the land (Ruth 1:1).
- The marriages of Naomi's sons produce no children (Ruth 1:3–7).
- Naomi alludes to her empty arms and empty womb (Ruth 1:11–12).
- Naomi bemoans the bitterness of her life (Ruth 1:13).
- "Don't call me Naomi," she told them. "Call me Mara, because the Almighty has made my life very bitter" (Ruth 1:20).
- "I went away full and the LORD has brought me back empty" (Ruth 1:21).

And then, the tide begins to turn:

Fruitfulness

- So Naomi returned from Moab accompanied by Ruth ... arriving in Bethlehem as the barley harvest was beginning (Ruth 1:22).
- So she went out and began to glean in the fields (Ruth 2:3).

- As she got up to glean, Boaz gave orders to his men, "Even if she gathers among the sheaves, don't embarrass her. Rather, pull out some stalks for her from the bundles and leave them for her to pick up, and don't rebuke her" (Ruth 2:15–16).
- Then she threshed the barley she had gathered, and it amounted to about an ephah. She carried it back to town and her mother-in-law saw how much she had gathered (Ruth 2:17–18).
- So Ruth stayed close to the servant girls of Boaz to glean until the barley and wheat harvests were finished (Ruth 2:23).
- "Bring me the shawl you are wearing and hold it out." When she did so, he poured into it six measures of barley and put it on her (Ruth 3:15).
- "He gave me these six measures of barley, saying, 'Don't go back to your mother-in-law empty-handed'" (Ruth 3:17).
- So Boaz took Ruth and she became his wife. Then he went to her, and the LORD enabled her to conceive, and she gave birth to a son" (Ruth 4:13).

For each of us, there are going to be periods of loss, sorrow, and barrenness in our lives. But the book of Ruth teaches us that God is faithful, and in due season if we do not give up, we will reap a harvest.

Famine doesn't always mean judgment, but because this was the Promised Land, God's people, and a story God chose to tell, we can be fairly certain that this drought was a judgment of God. God was looking for repentance.

Naomi's husband, Elimelech, instead of leading his family in repentance, tries to get around God. He takes his family to idol-worshipping Moab—where there is plenty of rain and food. (Numbers 25 will show you how depraved the people of Moab were.) When Elimelech arrives in Moab, he suddenly dies. (That doesn't mean that all people who die young are being judged by God or that Elimelech won't be in heaven. But it does seem God was displeased with his choice.)

Elimelech could have been a fairly decent man who simply buckled under pressure. We all do. It is one of the reasons we should not trust in men or in marriage for our security in life. Men (and women) buckle. God never does.

Especially as women—who are wired to be relational—we may be tempted to make people our gods. (Men often trust the false gods of position and money.) Our trust may be in a best girlfriend, a child—but more often, it is in a man.

In Naomi's day, women were truly destitute without a man. They could not own property, but were dependent on their fathers, husbands, or sons to care for them. Yet even then, God longed for women to put their trust in Him. Ruth did, as we will see, and God met her.

Though the status of women is far different today, we still seem to have the same propensity toward trusting in husbands. Many women still experience panic if they are single.

Senior Panic

When I was in college, I had a sorority sister whom I will call Jill. Jill was experiencing "senior panic." She had not found a man. To her great relief, during the spring, a man began dating her seriously. The only problem was that she didn't really like him. Nevertheless, they became engaged. I remember the astonishment I felt when Jill came back to my room after talking to her fiancé on the phone. She flopped on the bed and moaned, "Oh, Dee, I just hate the sound of his voice. It's whiny, nasal, and effeminate." And yet, she married him.

I think Naomi felt this panic for her daughters-in-law. It is evident she loved them. Yet when they wanted to go with her back to Bethlehem, she didn't want them to. Why? Read her words carefully:

> Go back, each of you, to your mother's home.... May the LORD grant that each of you will find rest in the home of another husband. (Ruth 1:8–9)

What I think Naomi was thinking, but was too kind to say, was:

> These girls will remain single if they come with me. What man in Bethlehem would want a Moabite girl? I've got to send them back so they can get a man.

Pastor John Bronson said, "Naomi had an opportunity to make an eternal difference in the lives of her daughters-in-law. If they came with her to Bethlehem, they might come to know the one true God. But she is so concerned about getting them married, she blows it."[4]

Naomi doesn't just send them back once. She actually tells them to go home three times! They weep, they cling to her—but she is adamant. She reiterates her reason.

> Why would you come with me? Am I going to have any more
> sons, who could become your husbands? (Ruth 1:11)

Naomi measured her worth on the basis of marriage and mother-hood, and she felt worthless. She felt she had nothing to offer these girls. (She actually had everything that mattered—a relationship with the one true God.) Three times she tells them to go back to Moab where they can get a man—for she cannot give them one. Orpah is finally con-vinced, for she kisses her mother-in-law good-bye and goes back, fading out of the pages of Scripture.

"Call Me Mara!"

An intriguing aspect of the book of Ruth is the meaning of each per-son's name. Elimelech's name means "My God is King." Even though Elimelech failed to bow his knee to his King, his God was still King. The Lord will be Lord whether we recognize Him or not. Orpah's name means "stiff-necked" or "double-minded." Her turning back to Moab is symbolic of turning back to the old way of life instead of taking the risk of faith. Ruth means "a woman friend," and she has a book in the Bible named after her! Naomi's name means "sweet" or "pleasant," but she feels abandoned by God and found her name to be cruelly ironic.

I cannot imagine a greater pain than that of the death of your hus-band *and* children. I empathize when Naomi cries, "Don't call me Naomi [sweet] ... Call me Mara [bitter] because the Almighty has made my life very bitter.... Why call me Naomi? The LORD has afflicted me; the Almighty has brought misfortune upon me" (Ruth 1:20–21).

I applaud her honesty, and I cannot be too judgmental of her despair. I myself have felt "frozen" since Steve died (eight months ago at this rewriting). Worship and time in the Word have not sprung from feelings of hunger, but from obedience and the knowledge that it would be foolish to back away from God. I know He is my only lifeline. But, like Naomi, I am telling God that I am hurting. I might as well tell Him, for He knows anyhow. Naomi's honesty in expressing her pain not only helped her to grieve, but let Ruth understand Naomi's deep need for a steadfast friend.

Luci Shaw, my friend and favorite poet, was widowed in midlife. Like Naomi, Luci was in pain. You could see it in her eyes. She described being widowed as "radical surgery—like being cut in half." Luci's reaction to pain has been a model to me. She says:

> I'm learning to welcome pain, and not to dodge it. It's one of the most valuable of lessons. Pain has a refining work to do in us, if we welcome it. It teaches us what is temporal, what is superficial, and what is abiding and deep. I'm trying to let pain do its work in me.[5]

Luci lived in a wooded suburb of Chicago. We walked together in her front yard and looked at the place where a large oak tree had stood. Her poetic mind, like that of our Lord's, often sees parabolic significance in the earthly, lifting it to the transcendent.

A week or so after her husband had died, the tree, ridden with disease, had to be toppled. In her freshly widowed pain, Luci had seen parallels between the screaming power saws and her husband's cancer, between the white-hot fire that burned the debris and stump for two days and his death. Finally, she herself identified with the black-rimmed ashen hole that was left like a wound in the frozen sod. As we stood there silently, I recalled words she'd written in an article:

> I was the frozen sod with the deep wound, and Harold was my tree who was simply ... gone. Vanished. How unreal it seemed that his roots, that had for over thirty years penetrated deep into my life, that had anchored us, joined us so solidly and securely, were being eroded by the fire of decay. The space above ground that for so long had been filled with his vertical strength and solidity and shape was empty; air had rushed in where, before, the towering trunk had outbranched to leaves.
>
> Now I lie in wait for spring, for the tissue of earth and the skin of sod—the beauty of green instead of the grey ashes of a spent fire—to fill in and heal over the naked scar. And it will. It will.
>
> But the oak tree stands strong and thriving and leafy in my memory, and no one can cut it down.[6]

Luci planted a sapling where the oak once stood, a symbol of hope, of the resurrection, of her husband's new life. I thought of this as I stood at my own husband's grave. Steve's grave is too new to be covered with grass, and the deer ate the tulip bulbs we planted, but the Lilies of the Valley that cover the Wisconsin woods behind him are now creeping in, surrounding his gravestone.

My son, J. R., reminded me: "Jesus is the Lily of the Valley." I thought, *Yes, Jesus. You are. You are the One who rose from the dead, who turns ashes into beauty, and who brings hope in the midst of despair. You are the Lily of the Valley—the Bright and Morning Star. Thank You for spreading this symbol of hope over my precious husband's grave.*

Don't Push Your Friends Away

Luci Shaw understood that even though there is a temptation to pull the blanket over your head in grief and to send everyone away, that she needed her friends desperately. In support of this conviction, Luci showed me her calendar, dotted with time for friends. "It doesn't take much time to go out for breakfast," she commented. "It doesn't interfere with one's work schedule. I need to make time for that contact. I would feel much more bereft without my friends."

In times of grief, we are apt to hear dark voices—voices that tell us we are no longer people of value, beloved by God. If we withdraw from friends, a common response to depression, then those voices have no competition. We need to be with compassionate women who will come alongside us and show us that we *are* lovable human beings, precious in God's sight and in their sight. If our friends don't come to be with us, we must take the initiative to ask for their company. Luci does this. She and author Karen Mains are good friends. Luci said:

> I'll call Karen, and say, "Do you feel like going to a matinee?" and she'll say, "Oh, I've been writing all weekend! Let's go!" That does wonders for me. It takes my mind off myself, and in the company of a friend we can see a meaningful movie.

Research by Daniel Levinson of Yale indicates that difficult times in life, such as midlife or the loss of a mate, are more successfully negotiated by those who have strong same-sex friendships. That is why women seem to cope better than men with the loss of a spouse.[7]

Dr. Beth Hess says, "There is a strong hypothesis that friends help women survive. Part of women's ability to sustain themselves in older years depends on their capacity for constructing a network of friends."[8]

Luci Shaw is also close to Madeleine L'Engle, brought together not only by an editorial relationship, but by many other bonds. Luci said, "I feel a sister to Madeleine in so many ways." I wrote to Madeleine L'Engle, asking her to reflect on her friendship with Luci. She responded:

> As an only child I depend on and rejoice in the sistership of many friends, such as Luci Shaw. The sisterhood of my friends involves an understanding that our Creator is good, and that our lives have meaning; also a loving forbearance of our humanness. Luci and I share much in our love of words as our expression of our love of the Word. And we have shared the illnesses and deaths of our lives' companions, and discovered God's grace and joy in the midst of pain.

Luci invited Madeleine to come and spend a few days with her in her West Chicago home while they worked together on the editing of Madeleine L'Engle's book *A Stone for a Pillow*. Despite the conflicts between editor and author (Madeleine is a controversial writer for many Christians), and despite the struggles that each were facing in their personal lives, both found great stimulation, camaraderie, and comfort in their multileveled relationship. Luci smiled as she remembered how Madeleine had closed a daylong editorial session. "When we were all done, Madeleine said, 'Now we shall rise and sing, "Praise God from Whom All Blessings Flow."' And we did."

Learning to Value Women As Much As Men

Naomi never expected to be left without men. If we, like Naomi, allow our sense of security and self-esteem to be based on a man's constant presence, then we are headed for trouble. Singles who embrace this fairy tale will miss the happy and fulfilled life God desires for them. Married women who embrace this fairy tale will fail to see the Lord as their Protector, Provider, and Confidante. Most will eventually become bitter, since widowhood, for those wives who don't divorce, is a statistical probability. According to 1983 U.S. census statistics, widows outnumber widowers five to one. [9]

Naomi also feels empty and worthless without men in her life. In fact, *empty* is the very word she uses when she arrives in Bethlehem and her old friends rush out to meet her. She says, "I went away full, but the Lord has brought me back empty" (Ruth 1:21).

Empty! How that must have hurt Ruth! The women of Bethlehem could see that Naomi hadn't come back empty. And as the days progressed, they could see what Naomi failed to see: That God had provided her with a real friend in Ruth. For Ruth was helpful and kind and good to her mother-in-law. There's a gentle rebuke at the end of the book when the women of Bethlehem tell Naomi, "Your daughter-in-law … loves you and … is better to you than seven sons" (Ruth 4:15).

Pastor John Bronson commented, "I wonder if Naomi shed a tear and blushed with shame to realize that God's blessing for her had been at her side from the very beginning."[10]

Peg's husband left her for another woman when their daughter was a baby. Peg said:

> For years I prayed for a father for Jamie. I felt so alone in raising her—I wanted someone with whom I could share not only my parenting problems, but also my joys! Recently it has occurred to me that although God has not given me a man, He has answered my prayer for Jamie, in a sense, in my dear girlfriend. Gay loves Jamie as if she were her own. She's terribly interested in all the little details of her life. And it is Gay to whom I go with my concerns and joys about Jamie.

God may choose to meet our needs through women, but if we value them less than men, we may not see it. There is still a tendency today to value men over women. And that was even truer in Ruth's day, for every woman belonged to some man as wife, daughter, or slave. When Naomi lost her men, she also lost her social standing. Yet when Ruth lost her man, she did not lose her sense of worth or her hope, because that was in God. Ruth was ahead of her time—and ours!

In an article on the book of Ruth, Jane Titterington writes,

> We need to be reminded that our value as human beings is something bestowed on us by God regardless of our marital status. Placing an inordinate value on the man-woman relationship tends to produce a rather warped view of humanity…. We see men as prey and other women as pawns to be used or rivals to be competed against in this game.[11]

Although there have been negative things in the women's movement, one positive effect is that women are beginning to truly value each other. One woman shared:

> All through college I had friends. Girlfriends were basically to pass the time until I had a real relationship, I thought.... It's only now I realize how happy just being with girlfriends made me and how much support they gave me through awful times, like trying to diet off twenty pounds, when they cheered each ounce I lost, or the time two of them stayed up all night with me, helping to type a paper. But there wasn't a time I wouldn't break a date with a friend if I got a chance to go out with a guy.... Only recently did I realize how important one special friend was in my life. Her name was Marlene and we roomed together my junior year. It was my happiest year of college, but I never credited Marlene for being the reason.... Women friends count. I thank the women's movement for teaching me that.[12]

Another woman can uniquely empathize with feminine circumstances. (I nearly punched a male doctor who leaned over me when I was in labor and said patronizingly, "Aw, c'mon, it doesn't really hurt that much.") Jane Titterington says, "Just as the hand needs the eye, it also needs the other hand."[13]

Menopause

I believe another factor magnified Naomi's sense of worthlessness. My calculations put her in the change of life. (She would have been close to forty when both sons were of marrying age, and close to fifty after they had been married ten years.) Menopause usually occurs between forty-five and fifty-five years of age.

Not only her age but her words give support to the theory that Naomi was menopausal. She tells Ruth and Orpah, in effect, that she is an "empty bag" with very little hope for conceiving more children. "I am too old! It's too late for me!"

This must have been particularly devastating to Naomi, whose only natural children had died. But Naomi wouldn't allow her women friends to comfort her. Instead she tried to send them away. "What I need," she must have thought, "is men—a husband and sons—not women!"

Menopause also, doctors tell us, can make a woman's emotions run rampant. The symptoms can be similar to those of premenstrual syndrome. In Hans Christian Andersen's fairy tale "The Snow Queen," there is a "horrid mirror in which all good and great things were magnified and every flaw became very apparent."[14]

Dr. James Dobson describes how menopause changed his mother from a joyful, peaceful woman to a woman who was extremely irritable and depressed for weeks at a time. Six physicians told her the problem was psychological. Yet when she began receiving estrogen treatments, her condition changed. We need help from the medical community, and we need understanding from each other.

We must believe the best about each other and realize that a friend's irritability may be a reaction to the chemistry in her body. One of the menopausal symptoms Dr. Dobson lists is "extremely low self-esteem, bringing feelings of utter worthlessness and disinterest in living."[15] This is how Naomi sounds when she calls herself "empty" and "without hope."

How much insight did Ruth and Orpah have into Naomi's behavior? It's intriguing to see how much they loved her in the face of her unloveliness. There must have been a time when Naomi was like her name, sweet and pleasant, loving Ruth and Orpah as if they were her own. They are determined to go with her to Bethlehem—willing to leave their own homes, people, and country just to be with Naomi! They do not intend to part from Naomi.

Yet after Naomi has told them to go home three times, Orpah retreats. (Most of us, if our mother-in-law told us three times to go home, would!) Orpah's reaction was natural.

Ruth's reaction was supernatural.

CHAPTER SIX

BINDING UP THE BROKENHEARTED

Intreat me not to leave thee, or to return from following after thee:
for whither thou goest, I will go; and where thou lodgest,
I will lodge: thy people shall be my people, and thy God my God.
Where thou diest, will I die, and there will I be buried: the LORD *do so to me,*
and more also, if ought but death part thee and me.

—RUTH 1:16–17 KJV

J gladly claim Ruth as a member of my sex. When Naomi was reject-
ing her, Ruth faced her squarely and said the words quoted above,
which have touched the souls of Christians and non-Christians alike.
She makes six promises, and then to convince Naomi she is serious, she
calls God's wrath upon her if she doesn't keep them.

The loveliness and the gravity of these vows take my breath away.
Vows made, not as the composers of wedding music would have us
believe, by a bride to her groom, but by one woman to another. What
a model of feminine friendship! Ruth shows us the height of which we,
as believing women, are capable, for God uses Ruth like a good medicine to restore an ailing Naomi.

In response to these vows, Naomi does not throw her arms around
Ruth and weep tears of gratitude. Instead, Naomi is silent. What is she
thinking? We find out when she and Ruth arrive in Bethlehem and
friends rush out, asking, "Can this be Naomi?" (It's only been ten years,
but bitterness has changed her appearance dramatically.)

Look again at Naomi's words from Ruth's perspective: "Don't call
me Naomi.... Call me Mara, because the Almighty has made my life

very bitter. I went away full, but the Lord has brought me back empty" (Ruth 1:20–21). Empty! And Ruth is right at her side.

If I had been Ruth, I would have been tempted to forget about my promises and turn around and go back to Moab where I might be more appreciated. But Ruth overlooks Naomi's words and gives her unfailing love like that of the Lord.

Do you see the fierce tension between Ruth and Naomi? John Bronson described it beautifully:

> Naomi says: "Go back!"
>
> Ruth says: "I will come."
>
> Naomi says: "I have no hope!"
>
> Ruth says: "My destiny is joined to yours."
>
> Naomi says: "I am not pleasant. I am bitter."
>
> Ruth says: "I choose you, Naomi."[1]

Then, at the very time that Naomi is testifying against her God, Ruth commits herself to that God. Bronson continued:

> Naomi says: "My God has witnessed against me and His hand has gone out against me."
>
> Ruth says: "My God is your God."[2]

How was Ruth able to overcome Naomi's rejection and stay at her side? And how did Ruth know Naomi's God was trustworthy when Naomi was testifying against Him?

I believe we witness here an intertwining of a woman's gift of intuition with the Holy Spirit's power.

Ruth's Intuition and the Holy Spirit's Power

Had Ruth been thinking only with her left brain, she might have come to the seemingly logical conclusion that Naomi didn't need her or want her. Had Ruth had more androgenic hormones, she might have responded to Naomi's attack with a counterattack. But Ruth read between the lines, somehow coming to the correct conclusion that she should not leave Naomi. She stayed calm and steadfast in her purpose. How fitting that *Ruth* means "a woman friend"!

Ruth also seemed to know intuitively, despite her mother-in-law's negative testimony, that the God of Israel was trustworthy. And God responded to Ruth's mustard seed of faith by flooding her with Holy Spirit power.

Paul was able to say, "Follow my example, as I follow the example of Christ" (1 Cor. 11:1). Ruth could legitimately say the same to women who wish to use their gift for friendship to bless the world in a redemptive way. Let's consider how we can bind up the brokenhearted by following in Ruth's steps.

Friends in Grief Need Empathy

Author Paula D'Arcy began keeping a diary during her pregnancy. She wrote "letters" to her baby, telling the child about all the wonderful feelings she was having in anticipating the birth. When Sarah was born, Paula continued her diary, recording the joy she and her husband, Roy, found in their daughter.

When Sarah was two, the family was coming home from a holiday and was hit head-on by a drunk driver. Roy and Sarah died in the hospital. The following letter from Paula's diary was written about a month after the tragedy:

> September, 1975
>
> Dear Sarah: I can't be polite to one more visitor. No one would like me if they knew what I really was thinking when they say how lucky I am that I wasn't badly injured. That I lived. The person I used to be would have understood their intentions....
>
> But today I can't pass off the words. This new person doesn't have energy left to do anything but stay alive and not scream. I don't want to hear anyone else's awkward attempts. They make me angrier than I already am.[3]

Paul exhorts us to "carry each other's burdens" (Gal. 6:2). The word he uses for burdens refers to the temporary *overburden* that a sister may be carrying, as distinct from the *everyday* load he refers to in Galatians 6:5. When we are temporarily overburdened due to the stress of death, divorce, illness, and so on, we definitely need the supportive help of our sisters. We need someone to come alongside and help shoulder the overburden.

The best way to do that is by empathizing, weeping with those who weep. Your quiet and listening presence will help absorb some of the pain and relieve some of the burden. If we attempt to deny the burden by pointing out blessings, we add to the pain. Solomon clarifies this with similes: "Like one who takes away a garment on a cold day, or like vinegar poured on soda, is one who sings songs to a heavy heart" (Prov. 25:20). Too much cheerfulness or the offering of solutions intensifies grief.

I understood this in part before my husband's illness, but oh, do I understand it now! Even condolence cards can twist the knife by giving you a little sermonette. When my husband was dying and suffering incredibly, I'd open up a card that said:

> All things work together for the good of those who love God and are called according to His purpose. (See Rom. 8:28.)

And I'd want to scream. *How insensitive,* I'd think. I know the above verse is true, but there is a time to speak it, and a time to be silent. High-tide grief calls for empathy, *not* solutions.

Women are usually better at empathizing than men. Women's feeling-oriented right brains overcome the left-brain response of coming up with solutions. "It's okay to hurt; it's okay to grieve," the right brain says.

During a discussion in our Sunday school class on marriage, wife after wife lamented that men's natural response to problems seemed to be to jump in and find solutions rather than provide comfort: "I don't want to hear how I could avoid this kind of pain in the future. I want to hear that he cares I'm hurting!" "I don't want any solutions. No advice. I want him to hold me tenderly and be quiet!"

I told the class that as a newlywed I had to teach Steve to put his arms around me and say simply, "Poor Dee Dee!" At this they laughed uproariously, and now the men tell us that when their wives are upset, they do exactly as I suggested. One man went so far as to say that he doesn't even say, "Poor Marsi!" to his wife, using her name, but "Poor Dee Dee!"

A study of 15,000 women by *Family Circle* found that 69 percent of women would rather talk to their best friends when they're feeling unhappy than to their spouses.[4] An interesting study on listening skills found that women are much more empathetic listeners. The sympathetic responses like "um-hmmm," and "go on" were recorded, and women far outdistanced men.[5] Most people who have been through a crisis find it therapeutic to go over and over the details. They need a listening, caring presence.

Elaina's husband left her and their daughter to pursue a gay lifestyle. Reflectively, Elaina said:

> After my divorce, I really felt like I'd been given a bum rap. If I hadn't had my women friends to pour out my heart to, I'd have killed myself. I was so caught up in my misery, I never asked them one question about themselves. I know I wasn't fun as a friend then—but they stood by me. I was a real drain, but they saw me through the long haul.

Don't Criticize the Person in Despair

Not only did Naomi fail to appreciate Ruth, she neglected her. It was dangerous for a foreign woman to glean in the fields, and Naomi should have steered Ruth toward the safer field of their near kinsman, Boaz. But Naomi was so overburdened, so immobilized by depression that she wasn't thinking of Ruth's needs.

Yet during this whole time, not one critical word flows from Ruth's mouth. Not one. Ruth simply comes alongside Naomi and quietly shoulders part of her burden. Naomi didn't need more judgment, but instead desperately needed to experience the goodness of the Lord. Ruth made that possible through her obedience and trust in Him.

Be Patient

How long do we carry an overburden for another? As long as necessary. Emily, whose teenage daughter drowned three years ago, said:

> I'm better now—I'm not thinking of Amy every waking moment. There are even days when I don't cry. But I still need a lot of support. Sometimes my mother will say, "It's time now to get past this." I can't take that. I understand she says that because it hurts her to see me hurting. But I still need Mom to simply open her arms and hold me.

I asked author Joe Bayly, who was acquainted with grief through the loss of three children, about a young friend of mine who had been widowed two years previously: "Is it time to tell her to stop grieving?" Eyes full of compassion, he shook his head. "Give her the time she needs."

One of the reasons I am eager for a person to get past her grief is that

I am weary of helping her carry her burden. Perhaps that is why Paul tells us a few sentences after telling us to bear one another's burdens, "Let us not become weary in doing good, for at the proper time we will reap a harvest if we do not give up" (Gal. 6:9).

We should stay alongside until we see restoration. The first glimmer of restoration occurs in Naomi when Ruth returns from the field of Boaz, arms overflowing with grain. Naomi brightens and asks, "Where did you glean today? Where did you work? Blessed be the man who took notice of you!" (Ruth 2:19).

When Ruth tells Naomi that she'd been in the field of Boaz, Naomi realizes for the first time in a long time that her God has not forgotten her. According to levirate law, Boaz has a responsibility toward them. In order to carry on the name of a married man who died childless, this law called for a near kinsman to marry the widow and raise up a child in his late kinsman's name.

Naomi realizes that God was involved in leading Ruth to the field of Boaz. With tears in her eyes, Naomi gives God the glory: "[The Lord] has not stopped showing his kindness to the living and the dead." She adds, "That man is our close relative; he is one of our kinsman-redeemers" (Ruth 2:20).

Hurting People May Not Ask for Help

Most of us are extremely reluctant to ask for help. And when we're injured (emotionally or physically), we tend to send people away when we need them the most! Like a man hanging on the edge of a precipice by his fingernails, we refuse the outstretched hand and say, "That's okay—I think I can make it."

Lynn waited all night for news of her boyfriend, Craig, who was the pilot of a missing emergency medical helicopter. When search teams found the wreckage and Lynn's worst fears were confirmed, she headed to the telephone and called her best friend, Susy. "Do you want me to come?" Susy asked. Lynn said,

> I told her, "It's not necessary—I'll be okay." Susy lived so far away; I didn't want to inconvenience her. I didn't realize how desperately I would need her when the shock wore off. Thank God she came.
>
> I also told my friend Deb to go on home after the helicopter

> was reported missing. She had worked a long shift, and I hated to
> make her stay—I knew it could be a long, long time. But she stayed
> all night. She was with me in the morning, when they told me
> they found the bodies. She cried with me and held me. I'll never
> forget that.

I asked Lynn what she thought a person should do if a good friend
tells her not to come during a time like this.

Lynn said, "If she's a good friend—*go!*"

If we are the ones who are hurting, we should remember that those
who truly love us *want* to help bear our burdens. Though it's hard to
admit we need help, we need to learn to do it. Luci Shaw told me about
a week in the year following her husband's death when she was very ill
with the flu:

> I was all alone in the house that week—my temperature soared to
> 103 degrees and I was drifting in and out of reality. I was so weak
> that I was really afraid of walking downstairs to get a ginger ale. I
> thought, "If I fall and break my leg, then I'll really be in trouble."

Luci finally decided to call her good friend Karen Mains from the
bedside phone to ask her to stop at a store and bring her something to
drink. "I knew she was busy, loaded—she had five broadcasts to do that
week! But I also knew that there was a supermarket near where she
worked and my home was near hers, so it wouldn't take too much of
her time."

Luci called and Karen wasn't there. Luci dared to persist by leaving
a message explaining her predicament. She smiled as she remembered
Karen's response:

> She breezed in and took over. She gave me popsicles and Gatorade,
> took my temperature, and gave me a cool rubdown. And you
> know, it made her feel contented and happy that a friend would
> feel free to call her. When friends are close, we don't need to fear
> to ask for help. If we could just realize that!

We need to overcome our reluctance in asking people to help us
bear our temporary overburdens. And we need to be discerning, like
Ruth, and realize that a friend may really need us despite her protesta-
tions otherwise.

Sometimes a friend in need doesn't ask for support because severe
depression has immobilized her. Chris, mother of three, has battled

with clinical depression for years. "I can't relate to people during those times because I don't even understand what is going on in my own head. But friends sustain me through cards, letters, and flowers—letting me know that they care about me when I don't care about myself."

The Multiplied Burden of Grief and Shame

When a woman loses a husband to death, the Christian community is better at coming alongside than when she loses a husband to divorce. Likewise, if a woman has a child who is desperately ill, her friends are there; but if she has a child who is involved with drinking or drugs, there really isn't the same support. We're hesitant to bring up the subject for fear of making our friend feel worse, but ironically, our silence may be misinterpreted as an accusation. We need to learn to say enough to show empathy and an open door if the person would like to talk or pray with us. There isn't one of us who couldn't be in her shoes, and we need to let her know that.

Sharon, a godly woman whose son had just been given a prison sentence, hugged me hard when I said, "I hear you're going through a rough time."

She said, "Oh, Dee, most people don't say anything."

When Adele's husband, who had been a pastor of a conservative church, became involved with another woman, Adele said that their Christian friends seemed to disappear from their lives. Adele said:

> I needed my friends so badly when Jim moved out, but they weren't really there. I wasn't able to ask them to come and spend time with me, for it's extremely difficult for a hurting person to verbalize a need for help. After the divorce was final, people would tell me, "When I knew there was a problem, I wanted to come to see you, but I didn't know what to say. So I didn't come." And my heart cried out within me, "Oh, if only you had just come!"

When her husband left her, Adele's value as a person had been attacked. I asked Adele what kinds of things she would have asked for, had she been able—and she gave me a list! So that we can better reach out to our friends, this deserves posting on the refrigerator.

- Contact the person often. Call. If you don't know what to say, ask, "How is your day going?" Write a note showing you care. Stop by. (I felt so isolated. I kept the cards people sent on my piano. Looking at them strengthened me to face the day.)

- Invite them to share a normal activity with you: a walk, a sporting event, an errand, a meal.
- Sit with them in church. They feel unworthy to join you. Don't let them sit there alone.
- Touch them, hug them. (I am hungry for touch. I miss the physical touch of one who cares.)
- Identify with their feelings. Don't be afraid to mention the other party by name. (A friend of mine saw me cutting the lawn and asked, "Did Jim used to cut the lawn?" Just mentioning him made me feel freer to talk to her.)
- Pray with them. And daily pray for them! Put their name on your mirror so you don't forget!

A Time to Speak

Solomon tells us there is a time to be silent and a time to speak (Eccl. 3:7). All through this chapter I've been encouraging you to exercise your feminine gift for empathy, and I've stressed that the person in grief doesn't need solutions or confrontation, but your empathizing presence.

But there are times when we must speak up. If we make the mistake of quietly empathizing when we should be alerting our friend to danger, we may actually be holding her hand as she walks toward the cliff.

I was convicted by an observation Christian counselor Jay Adams makes in *Competent to Counsel*. He says that too often when a friend makes a comment like, "I guess I haven't been much of a mother or a wife," we respond by minimizing her confession. We'll say, "Don't talk like that, Susie; you know you haven't been that bad." I've done this—even if I know Susie is a terrible wife or mother! This is a destructive use of my feminine gift for empathy.

Adams says it would be much more productive to say, "Well now, that's a serious matter before God; how have you failed as a wife?"[6]

Likewise, I'm sure Satan is pleased when we fail to speak up and expose his deception when we suspect a friend is considering divorce, an abortion, an affair, or marriage to an unbeliever.

Galatians 6:1 tells us, "Brothers, if someone is caught in a sin, you who are spiritual should restore him gently." How can you confront gently? By helping her discover how this sin will hurt her.

Christian psychiatrist Louis McBurney finds that when dealing with those considering divorce, taking "a hard-line, frontal assault with Scripture verses flying only increases defensiveness and resistance."[7] He has better results when he examines the world's view that divorce is a "quick relief." Gently he shows them that "after the initial relief, most people face a period of grief for a year or more."[8] Only a small percentage of individuals, ten years later, are glad they divorced. (There are exceptions, however—and we need to be alert that *some* desperately need encouragement to set boundaries so that their mate might get the help he needs for addictions, abuse, or infidelity. Sometimes he will refuse and this will lead to the end of a marriage.)

Divorce is often chosen, not because of scriptural reasons, but because of selfishness. Sometimes caring questions can help the person begin to think more realistically about the effect of her choice: "If you go ahead with this divorce, what do you think your life will be like financially? If you have this abortion, what kind of thoughts do you think you will have about this baby in years to come? If you marry Joe [an unbeliever], will you go to church alone?" Gently steer her toward a realistic view of the long-term consequences of her choice.

If you are close to the person and have all the facts (unfortunately, it is often acquaintances who confront and close friends who stay mum), then God may very well be calling you to go, in a spirit of gentleness, and help your friend see what the consequences of her sin could be.

We should confront when we think it might save our friend from disaster. But sometimes it's too late for confrontation. The damage has been done: the marriage vows have been spoken; the divorce is final; the abortion has been committed; the money has been gambled away in the commodities.

In the play, "A Raisin in the Sun," there's a scene I'll never forget. Walter has lost all of the family's savings, savings that were going to make this family's dream come true. Now the dream has dried up like "a raisin in the sun." Beneatha is so disgusted with her brother that she says, "There ain't nuthin' left to love."

In a climactic, emotion-filled moment, Mama puts her hands on her daughter's shoulders, looks her directly in the eyes, and says:

> Child, when do you think is the time to love somebody the most;
> when they done good and made things easy for everybody? Well,
> then, you ain't through learning—because that ain't the time at
> all. It's when he's at his lowest and can't believe in hisself 'cause
> the world done whipped him so.[9]

Ruth is a model to me, not just in the way she restored Naomi, but in another important way. This characteristic of Ruth, which I deal with in the next chapter, will show you how to make a friend and develop friendships of depth.

Walter Wangerin, author of *The Book of the Dun Cow,* told Margaret Smith, "You like to jump into a friendship and not start at the beginning but in the middle." She said, "That's exactly right!" And I agree. Who wants to go through the boring preliminaries? If I can avoid them, I will! And Ruth is showing me how.

CHAPTER SEVEN

THE RISK OF LOVE

*The risk of love
is that of being unreturned.
For if I love too deep,
too hard, too long
and you love me little
or you love
me not at all
then is my treasure given,
gone,
flown away lonely.*

*But if you give me back
passion for my passion,
return my burning,
add your own
dark fire to flame my heart
then is love perfect
hot, round, augmented,
whole, endless, infinite,
and it is fear
that flies.*[1]

—LUCI SHAW

*I*ntimacy is risky. No doubt about it. If I reach out to a woman to whom I am drawn, she may reject me. If I tell a woman that I love her, that I cherish her as a friend, she may respond little (or not at all). If I open my soul to another, trusting her with my dark side of failure, she may draw back in shocked silence (or she may tell others). Risky. Risky. Risky.

Then why do it? Why set ourselves up for hurt? Why not play it safe, as most men do? Because daring to take risks, as Ruth did, ignites the flame for bonding. In Sunday school many of us were told, "Dare to be a Daniel!" Perhaps we should be telling girls, "Risk being a Ruth!"

Risk Reaching Out

There was a time when a newcomer to the neighborhood was heralded as a joyous event. Those nearby embraced them with visits, gifts of food, and genuine interest. Not so today.

Kathleen said, "The first two months after moving from Texas, my phone bill to friends back home was astronomical. I figured I'd write it off as a medical deduction!"

I identify with Kathleen. When we moved from Seattle to a suburb of Portland, Oregon, I too felt the anxiety of being separated from my women friends. It didn't help that it rained—steadily—for the first three weeks. (I was beginning to have great empathy for Noah!) No cheery neighbor braved the rain with a plateful of chocolate chip cookies. The gloom outside my window augmented the gloom in my spirit. If I wanted a friend, I was going to have to take the initiative.

I began to plead unrelentingly with the Lord for a local sister in Christ who could be my friend. (And I have found that when my prayers are in earnest, then I am much more alert for the Lord's response.)

Knowing that group Bible study is usually a good source for friends, I decided to try Bible Study Fellowship, a national interdenominational organization. Portland's group happened to be meeting in a large church in our suburb.

One Tuesday morning I drove up to the church in a downpour. I was astounded by the number of cars. Every space in the huge parking lot was taken, as were any available spaces on the streets near the church. I parked three blocks away and ran sloshing through the puddles, trying to hurry while avoiding the earthworms that had crawled out for air.

I walked through the double doors to hear the singing already in progress, acutely aware that I was late. The sanctuary was packed to overflowing with women. Somehow the camaraderie of the crowd made me feel lonelier than ever.

I was going to slip into one of the chairs set up at the back for latecomers when a beautiful woman in the center section, front pew, caught my eye. She had the clean look that blondes without bangs have, her long platinum hair pulled back in a neat, thick braid. *Why do I feel so drawn to her?* I wondered. *Is it simply because she is so attractive? Or is it possible that the Holy Spirit is drawing my attention to her? Is she the friend for whom I've been praying?*

If God was leading me, I was going to have to walk in my wet and bedraggled state in front of everyone in order to sit next to her. All the way across. Risky. Maybe crazy. But so intense was my need for a friend that I did it.

She looked up from her hymnal, startled by my presence.

(She looked so sophisticated—so dry!) But she smiled reassuringly, moved over to give me room, and shared her hymnal. I felt hopeful until the singing and the lecture ended and she left, without a word, to go to her small group. I stayed with a handful of newcomers to get my instructions. We filled out some forms and then were dismissed early, being told we would be assigned to regular small groups the next week. No one spoke to me personally. I went home, feeling lonelier than before I came.

I did risk going back, however. I didn't see the tall, cool blond until we divided into our small groups. I was assigned to room 101, the room for those whose last names began with letters Br through Ca. When I walked in, I was surprised to see her, seated at a round table with nine other women. (I wondered, *Providence or coincidence?*) Her name was Pam Carlson. When she saw me, her face didn't register recognition. (I do look different, however, when I'm not dripping wet.)

Reserved, Pam spoke only once during the whole hour, but then with an earnestness and insightfulness that stilled the room. She was an intent listener, leaning forward in her chair, making eye contact with whomever was speaking. *There are so few good listeners,* I thought, and remembered how C. S. Lewis had said in *Mere Christianity* that *that* might be one of the first things you notice in a genuine believer. Most people are so caught up in themselves that they are not good listeners—but Jesus can change that.

At one point, when a description of the crucifixion was read from Scripture, Pam's eyes filled with tears. I felt coldhearted in comparison. Pam hadn't lost her first love. Again, I felt drawn to her. Again, I determined to risk reaching out to her.

After the study, Pam swept up her books and darted out the door. Determined, I charged after her. I fell into step with her in the church parking lot. I told her I appreciated the comment she'd made. (I was hoping she'd realize this was an overture of friendship.) But instead our conversation took a nosedive as she said, "Thank you! See you next week!" and ran toward her car, leaving me standing alone, slightly embarrassed.

I chastised myself. *You're behaving foolishly. God is not leading and Pam is not interested in being your friend.* I decided to abandon my wild goose chase while I still had dignity. (Had I been familiar with Ruth's persistence in the face of rejection, I might have been stronger.) But just as I was about to give up, God intervened.

Steve and I had tried four different churches during our first month in Oregon. None of them seemed right for us. That Sunday we decided to visit a small church in the country. When we walked in the door, Pam saw me before I saw her. She and her husband were the official greeters. "Dee!" she called out to me. I turned, surprised that anyone would know my name. When I saw her, I had the sensation you have when you realize the pieces are fitting together and you know God is answering prayer. Encouraged, I asked Pam if she could come over for coffee the next day. She smiled warmly and said, "I'd love to!"

With kindred spirits, with a friendship given to you by God, it *is* possible to jump in at the "middle of a friendship." You can begin with personal issues right away. Before I had even poured coffee for Pam, she asked me, "How did you come to Christ?" She was an active listener, prodding me with questions. Then she told me her story.

On a lark, Pam had gone with some women from work to a Billy Graham crusade. On the way home her friends were laughing, ridiculing Dr. Graham. Pam alone was silent, thinking seriously about the reality of Jesus Christ. The Holy Spirit was at work. Compelled, Pam went back the next night and gave her life to Christ. Her sincerity was evidenced by the fact that she and her husband were taking in troubled teenage foster boys, eager to share the overflow of love they'd both found in Christ. I was impressed and encouraged by her lifestyle of obedience.

Pam risked opening herself up to me, telling me of her struggle to live simply. "I love nice things—and they have a giant grip on my mind and heart." We talked about how we thought a Christian *should* live, if he's not being squeezed into the world's mold. Then Pam broke the intensity of our discussion and sent us into gales of laughter by commenting, "I'm so glad I got my antiques before I was saved!"

Pam and I were finishing the other's sentences, eager to press on to the height of our thoughts. Author Randolph Bourne said, "One comes from friends ... with a high sense of elation and the brimming adequacy of life ... the keen thoughts, the trains of arguments, the pregnant thoughts that spring so spontaneously to mind."[2]

God knew how Pam and I would mesh, how we could sharpen each other, and He had given us the gift of friendship. We both thrilled in discovering it.

Since my experience with Pam early on in my Christian walk, I have been more willing to risk reaching out to someone to whom I am drawn. Even if she is not initially responsive, if I think the Lord may be leading, I will risk again.

Start in the Middle

There's an art to skipping the superficial and beginning a friendship in the middle, and it's tied to asking questions. Pam and I asked each other how we had come to Christ. Ruth asks upon first meeting Boaz, "Why have I found such favor in your eyes that you notice me—a foreigner?" (Ruth 2:10). She's really asking him why he is drawn to her—an amazingly open and searching question—and Boaz, in responding, intimately affirms her.

I've found that with a new acquaintance or an old friend, our conversation goes much deeper, faster, if I ask, "What concerns have been on your heart lately?" Or, "What have you been thinking about lately?" rather than, "How are you?" With a friend who is a believer, we'll often share our hearts and then pray together. And praying with a friend bonds you faster than anything I know.

One author suggests some wonderful questions to ask people about their vocations: "Tell me what it takes to do a job like yours with excellence. What are the great challenges a person faces? Where do you confront ethical and moral questions?"[3]

The God Hunt

An exercise that has stood the test of time in provoking meaningful discussions is one Karen and David Mains introduced when they had their radio program, *The Chapel of the Air.* They suggested keeping a daily record (in your journal or on a pad on the refrigerator) describing how you've "spied" God in your life that day. Perhaps you spied an answer to prayer or timing that seems too perfect to be coincidence. Or, as you reflect on your day, you may remember a sunset that awed you or a friend who gave you comfort or grace. By keeping a notebook and mentally walking through your day, you are going to "spy" God where you might have missed Him. Not only is this a tremendous encouragement spiritually, but it's also a wonderful conversation starter with believing friends. You will bond together and sharpen each other in the Lord as you share the ways you've spied God in your life. Ask them to share a time when they were very aware of God's presence, help, or timing. It works every time.

Risk Making Yourself Vulnerable

My bonding with Pam was hastened by our willingness to strip away pretense. Ruth told her mother-in-law "everything" about her night with Boaz (Ruth 3:16). C. S. Lewis wrote, "Eros will have naked bodies; Friendship naked personalities."[4]

Women seem more willing to make themselves vulnerable than men. One semester my husband and I decided to abandon our team teaching of adult Sunday school and each lead a class with members of our own sex. Our reasoning was that people might feel freer to make themselves vulnerable when the opposite sex was absent. "It will be great," I assured my hesitant husband.

And my class *was* great. In three weeks the women were sharing openly, weeping, and hugging.

Steve's class, however, bombed. The men stayed on the surface, unwilling to talk about personal struggles or feelings. Steve concluded that he no longer wanted to teach a class that was exclusively male because, "a class needs women. Women are almost always the ones to risk saying what is really on their hearts. Once they begin, they act as a catalyst and there is genuine sharing from both sexes."

Our lack of inhibition in making ourselves vulnerable is one of the main reasons I am convinced that women have real friends. Ruth and Naomi might have stayed on an "in-law" basis had Ruth held Naomi at arm's length. But she never did. When asked about her night with Boaz, Ruth told her mother-in-law everything!

Vulnerability hastens bonding. Charlotte explained it like this: "When a woman friend confides in me, I feel honored, esteemed that she would trust me so."

Jim, an executive from Milwaukee, told me that he thinks it is easier for women to make themselves vulnerable to each other because there will be reciprocation. Who wants to disrobe before someone who gawks judgmentally and refuses to disrobe himself?

Though we are better at being open than men, we're still too cautious with trusted friends. We have some stripping to do. Authors Ann and Jan Kiemel would tell you that though they were twins, and sisters in Christ as well, it took them many years to appreciate the value of making themselves vulnerable to each other. Ann admits that she had the mistaken idea that people wouldn't like her if she told them bad things about herself. Ann writes: "Jan started to be honest and vulnerable before I did.... As I watched her, I began to see that being vulnerable actually draws people to us, because the world is full of people ... that are bleeding and hurting."[5]

Sometimes we are hesitant to risk vulnerability because we fear our listener might not keep our confidence. This can be a healthy fear. Ruth was open with Naomi because she trusted her. Solomon warns us: "A gossip betrays a confidence; so avoid a man who talks too much" (Prov. 20:19). A man or a woman who talks too much is less likely to be able to keep a rein on confidences. Author Gail MacDonald says, "I usually find if a person easily talks about other people in a negative way, I can assume she's going to do the same thing about me."[6] There are women, however, who can be trusted.

Vulnerability not only hastens bonding, it can embolden a hurting person to open a festering wound that needs to be opened. A godly woman told me, "Sometimes, when I am aware that it would be helpful to a friend to open up to me about a problem, but sense hesitancy, I'll lead the way by making myself vulnerable. I'll share where I am hurting or failing." This kind of risk-taking springs from a heart that is seeking the other's best, a heart longing to live a life pleasing to God.

Risk Following God's Leading

The most striking example of Ruth's risk-taking occurs when Naomi proposes a daring plan to her daughter-in-law. First, Naomi tells Ruth to wash and perfume herself and dress in her best clothes. (That's the easy part.) Then she is to take note of where Boaz sleeps, guarding the grain, on the threshing-room floor. Under the cover of the black Bethlehem sky, unstained by modern city lights, Naomi tells Ruth to slip out, tiptoe up to the sleeping Boaz, uncover his feet, and lie down! Ruth responds like a dream daughter-in-law: "I will do whatever you say" (Ruth 3:5).

Why was Ruth so cooperative? It is characteristic of Ruth's life to take risks. However, she doesn't take random risks—she risks when she thinks God is leading.

I suspect that Naomi explained this all more thoroughly to Ruth, but we are not privy to the whole conversation. The symbolism behind this strange request is fascinating. To understand it, remember that Boaz was Naomi's "kinsman-redeemer." God set up a plan in His law to provide care for widows without sons. He designated a "rescuer" who was called the "kinsman-redeemer." If the late husband had a brother or a near relative, then that kinsman was supposed to redeem the property for the widow and redeem the family name by marrying the widow and raising up the first son in her late husband's name. In this case, Naomi was too old to have a child, so she wanted Ruth to act as her substitute. Boaz doesn't know this, so Naomi acts as a "coach," explaining to Ruth how to subtly communicate this to Boaz.

Why hasn't Boaz proposed to Naomi? It may have been because there was a nearer relative who was first in line and Boaz expected *this* man to fulfill the role. (In fact, when Ruth comes to Boaz as Naomi's substitute, the first thing Boaz does is to talk to this closer relative. This man refuses to rescue, not wanting a woman young enough to bear a son who would then grow up to inherit the property.) It is also possible that Boaz didn't approach either Naomi or

Ruth because he was shy around women. He's older, apparently single, and yet delighted when Ruth comes to him.

In *Anne of Green Gables,* Anne asks Matthew, her elderly guardian, if he ever went out with a girl, and he says, "No."

"Why ever not?"

Blushing, Matthew says, "Well, I couldn't do it without talking to a girl."[7]

Perhaps Boaz felt shy around women, especially a lovely young woman like Ruth. It was one thing to be kind to her, like a daughter, and quite another to propose marriage!

Does this mean it is okay for a girl to help out a shy guy? Though it seems Scripture calls men to be initiators, I think the Golden Rule calls for us to consider how hard that can be for someone who is shy and to encourage him by being warm and approachable. How far does that go? One woman told me: "I decided, on the basis of this passage, that it was okay for me to at least let it be known I'm available and interested—so I signed up for eHarmony." That's an interesting application, and not necessarily a wrong one, but I'm also positive it's not the central point of this passage.

The meaning behind this passage isn't so much about Ruth and Boaz, but about whom they represent. Ruth represents you and me, for we, like Ruth, were "aliens and strangers," in need of rescuing. Boaz represents Christ, who drew Ruth through his kindness, and as the "kinsman-redeemer" is the one who was able to rescue.

You see, Jesus is *our* Kinsman-Redeemer. He is our Kinsman in that He is fully man and is related to us. He is our Redeemer in that He was able to rescue us. In fact, we have only one Kinsman-Redeemer, for Christ alone was without sin so therefore able to cover us with His righteousness. He has drawn us to Himself as Boaz drew Ruth. When we go to the Lord and humbly "kneel at His feet" and cry, "cover me," He will respond as Boaz did to Ruth: "And now, my daughter, do not fear. I will do for you all that you request ..." (Ruth 3:11 NKJV).

Cover Me

When Ruth goes to Boaz that pivotal night and risks asking him to "cover her," or as some translations say, "take your maidservant under your wing," she is asking him to be her husband—to protect and provide for her. Husbands, in a mysterious way, foreshadow the ultimate Husband (Jesus) who protects and provides.

Many of you have heard me tell the story of my friend Jill, whose story parallels Ruth's. Her first husband, a young farmer, was killed in a terrible farming accident, leaving Jill alone with their four small children. Though Jill didn't want to leave the farm, it seemed impossible to stay, so she moved into the city with her children. Yet four years later God provided Jill a "Boaz" who truly loved her and the children.

He told Jill, "You are the family I thought passed me by." He married Jill, has been a real father to the children, and made it possible for them all to move back to that farm. (When Kathy Troccoli visited me in Nebraska, she wanted to meet Jill's husband, explaining, "I've met a lot of bozos, but never a Boaz!") A good husband is a foreshadowing of our ultimate Bridegroom, Jesus. He protects. He provides. He takes His bride under His wing.

God is angry with husbands who fail to "cover their wives." In Malachi 2 we see this clearly when there is a group of Israelite husbands who have chosen to be unfaithful with pagan women. They have cast their original wives aside, not even giving them the courtesy of a certificate of divorce. (Without that, the women could not remarry but were reduced to begging or prostitution.) Yet it is still church as usual, for the unfaithful husbands have come to temple to offer sacrifices. God is so angry—you can almost see the smoke and feel the temple shake. Yet when God refuses to receive the men's sacrifices, they seem clueless, and petulantly ask, "Why?"

God tells them they have failed to "cover" their wives with protection and provision. Instead, they have "covered" their wives with violence! There are a lot of subtle word plays in the Hebrew—including the idea that they are trying to "cover" their sin.

It's an important passage that, unfortunately, has often been misunderstood. It is in this passage where God also tells these unfaithful men that He "hates divorce." Unfortunately, this verse is often ripped out of context and used to make the victim feel guilty when God actually directed it to the one who was unfaithful. How we fail our sisters (or brothers) in Christ when they have been a victim of treachery, have been "cast aside" for another, and then are shamed by the church. Instead of shaming them, we should be encouraging them, telling them, "You can forgive your husband because God makes it very clear that He is angry with him, hates the divorce your husband has caused, and will deal with him."

Though this woman has been forsaken by her earthly husband, Jesus will never leave or forsake her—and neither should the church. We have also, to our shame, at times made a woman feel like she cannot separate from an unfaithful or abusive man, when that is exactly what God would have her do. Often that is the only thing that might bring him to his senses and have him get the help he and the marriage desperately need.

A failure to protect and provide for your family is shameful. Paul says a man like that is worse than an infidel (1 Tim. 5:8). There is even a shameful ceremony for the "kinsman-redeemer" who fails to cover the widow of his kinsman. According to Deuteronomy 25:9, Boaz would have had every right to spit in the nearer kinsman's face when that kinsman refused to fulfill his role. (I think Boaz was too happy, however, to spit in anyone's face! The way had been cleared for him to marry the woman of his dreams!)

Understanding all this helps us to realize why Naomi told Ruth to go and wake Boaz in the night and ask him to "cover her." Can you imagine how risky this must have felt? It is night. Boaz is guarding the grain against thieves. If anyone saw her, they might have jumped to the wrong conclusions. Yet Ruth was willing to do it in order to follow what she perceived as God's leading.

Boaz is fast asleep, when he suddenly senses a presence. Instead of leaping on what could have been an intruder, he asks, "Who are you?"

"I am your servant Ruth," she said. "Spread the corner of your garment over me, since you are a kinsman-redeemer" (Ruth 3:9). He understands instantly, praises Ruth, and then sets out to skillfully handle the nearer kinsman.

One of the things I love about the book of Ruth is that it is filled with "woman talk." There is such an excitement between Ruth and Naomi over Boaz and his responses. You can see it when Ruth came home the first night from the field of Boaz, and the two women practically get each other into a fever pitch, so great is their excitement. Now can't you just imagine Naomi waiting with anticipation for Ruth to return after approaching Boaz? When Ruth returns, again, with her arms *full* of grain, she tells her mother-in-law *everything*. It is wonderful to see Naomi so restored, trusting God, and believing that He will indeed work through Boaz. Ruth's friendship has been the means through which God restored Naomi's faith.

And God certainly does work through Boaz, who handles the sticky situation with the nearer kinsman with faith, diplomacy, and manly confidence. After the nearer kinsman refuses Ruth, Boaz announces to everyone that Ruth will be his wife, and that he will perpetuate the name of the late family. He says, "Today you *are* witnesses!" (Ruth 4:10). The "man of standing" (Ruth 2:1) is marrying "the woman of noble character" (Ruth 3:11). What a romance! Jesus is our "man of standing," and we are "women of noble character" because of Him.

At the festivities, the elders offer a lovely prayer not only for fertility, but for the name of the descendants to become famous in Bethlehem. God answers this prayer by "enabling Ruth to conceive," and she gives birth to Obed, who becomes the grandfather of David, King of Israel. So Ruth, a Gentile of Moabite background, has her name listed in the genealogy of Jesus! (See Matt. 1:5.) God had said that no Moabite would enter the assembly of the Lord even down to the tenth generation (Deut. 23:3), but our Lord no longer sees Ruth as a Moabite. She is a new creation; her past has been wiped away.

Author and speaker Win Couchman asked me, "Don't you think Ruth has a merry spirit?" How true! Never does she protest, "Oh, not that— think of the possible consequences!" In leaving Moab, in committing herself to Naomi and Naomi's God, in following Naomi's plan, she trusts God. Because she is persuaded that God is faithful, she risks everything over and over again. Consistent with her spirit, in the closing verses of the book, we see Ruth putting her baby into Naomi's empty arms. She shares eagerly, for she is not dependent on a man, a friend, or a child, but leans completely on God. He is faithful, blessing her with His power and presence and with earthly friendships. Her life is fruitful, as ours will be if we trust as she did.

Ruth's model shows me that it is possible to have a very close friendship and still be dependent on God. Perhaps Ruth passed this truth on to Obed, and he to Jesse, and he to David. For like his great-grandmother, David shows us how to be knit to a friend and yet be dependent on God alone.

CHAPTER EIGHT

BEST FRIENDS

*I've dreamed of meeting her all my life ... a bosom friend—an intimate friend,
you know—a really kindred spirit to whom I can confide my inmost soul.*[1]

—*ANNE OF GREEN GABLES*

*E*ach time my husband and I moved, I was restless until I found a
woman who could be the kind of friend that Anne Shirley
described in *Anne of Green Gables*. Though my husband was my dearest
friend, I had a longing for a special woman friend to whom I could confide my inmost soul. Best friendships reflect, most clearly, the gold in
the friendships of women—but also the dross. I would give my very life
for a best friend, but I could also become as petulant as a jilted lover
when a soul mate withdrew for a season. Lillian Rubin says, "Best
friends have the power to help and to hurt in ways that no one but a
mate or a lover can match."[2]

Naomi has shown me why I am so vulnerable. Like Naomi, I have a
tendency to depend on my human relationships rather than on God. I
have set myself up for pain, for even the dearest friend may betray me
or move away or die. Naomi has shown me my folly, but David and
Jonathan have modeled for me just how to prune away this ugly weed
of dependency.

David and Jonathan were knit together, but it was in a threefold cord
with God. We're told that Jonathan helped David find strength in God
(1 Sam. 23:16). Gail MacDonald says we need to ask, "Do you drive your
friend to God or to you? Are your friends dependent on you or are they
drawn to God?"

Dream Dreams for Your Best Friends

One of the ways we can drive a friend to God as David and Jonathan did is by dreaming dreams for her—dreams that will help her grow toward her potential in Christ.

My friend Pat encouraged me to send a Bible study I'd written for a small group of women to a publisher. When I resisted, she pushed! Her persistence was the beginning of my writing career. Do you see talents and gifts in your friend? Do you dream dreams of how she could more fully use them?

Listen to what Jonathan dreams for David: "Don't be afraid.... My father Saul will not lay a hand on you. You will be king over Israel, and I will be second to you" (1 Sam. 23:17).

Speak the Truth in Love

It is so hard to receive criticism, but if you can't, you are showing one of the prime characteristics of a fool, according to Proverbs. Understandably, it is easier to receive criticism from someone who really loves you, but even then, it is always hard to listen to something that will bring you pain.

Jonathan didn't *want* to believe that his father was trying to murder David. Yet when David rebuked Jonathan for being naïve about his father, Jonathan responded like a wise man, listening carefully. Jonathan wanted the truth, even if it hurt, and the truth enabled him to save David's life.

I believe that one of the purposes for best friendships is to help one another recognize blind spots. One of my closest friends, whom I will call Sharon, is married to an unbeliever—a man who crudely belittles Sharon's faith. Sharon once confided in me, "Dee, I don't want to sleep with him anymore. His language and his hardheartedness toward God turn me off."

I could empathize, but I also knew she shouldn't be shutting him out of their bed. I showed her the passage about not refusing one another sexually (see 1 Cor. 7:3–5). I remember that tears of conviction sprung to her eyes. She told me, months later, "Thank you for speaking the truth to me. I certainly wasn't being the kind of wife who would win her husband." Sharon is a wise woman who can receive criticism.

I long to have a teachable heart. Kathy Troccoli and I teach together—and we have often had to speak the truth in love to each other, for we each have blind spots. We are *so* different. God made me a teacher who longs to make the truths of God clear to women. God made Kathy an exhorter, and she passionately prepares and penetrates hearts. Kathy keeps things lively, often surprising me in the midst of a presentation with good-natured teasing or an amazingly funny quip. She worries that I am too stiff—I worry that she is having so much fun that the truth of God is being missed.

The first time Kathy started teasing me in the middle of a presentation I couldn't think! I lost my place and couldn't remember what to say next. Afterwards she confronted me. "Dee—you *have* to loosen up. Go with the flow. When you get rattled, it rattles the whole audience. If you will relax and laugh, then the audience will too. God *uses* humor to open up their hearts to the truth. Let it happen!"

I *have* learned—and now we have fun on stage and in the video curricula we've made together. And she's right: When the audience is relaxed—when they are connecting with you—their hearts become tender. And then, when the sword of God comes out, it slips right into a soft heart.

When Kathy and I were filming *Living in Love with Jesus,* I was making the point that God's commandments were not meant to steal our joy, but to enhance it! Sexual faithfulness, for example, can enhance a couple's sexual pleasure. Pretty soon Kathy had me *so* loosened up I was telling them about a plate I had made for Steve to carry at potlucks when we were young. It said,

> Rejoice in the wife of your youth ...
> let her breasts satisfy you at all times.
> (See Prov. 5:18–19.)

The audience was roaring, I was blushing, Kathy was teasing. Afterwards I pleaded with Russ, our producer, "Please, Russ—have mercy on me. Cut that scene!"

He laughed, "Oh, no. Not *one* second goes! That was the best part of the whole video."

I am a better teacher because I have loosened up—and I am thankful to Kathy for speaking the truth in love to me.

In the same way, Kathy has received my criticisms with an open and teachable heart. When I told her that I was concerned about having humor in the really serious parts, she *completely* stopped kidding me during those times. She said, "You have respected my anointing—I need to respect yours. Sometimes," she said sweetly, "you have to rein me in." People who have seen us work together often comment on how they see us growing stronger as a team. We smile at each other, knowing it has taken sweat and tears to get to this point.

Make Sacrifices to Help Her Realize Her Potential

Amy said, "Katherine and I led a women's Bible study together. Katherine is extremely gifted—and much more experienced than I. Yet she stepped aside and gave me the reins, because she wanted to encourage the gift she saw in me."

In Jonathan and David's greeting scene we're told, "Jonathan took off the robe he was wearing and gave it to David, along with his tunic, and even his sword, his bow and his belt" (1 Sam. 18:4). Jonathan, though he was next in line for the throne, believed David was the man in God's plan to be king of Israel. His gifts were symbolic of this; he was saying, "Let me make it clear, friend. All that I have is yours—even my right to the throne."

One sacrifice we each need to make for a best friend is space—space that gives her time for ministry. My friend Shell and I hold each other accountable for spending time with the lost and lonely, even though we often would prefer to spend that time with each other. We are committed to help each other live obediently.

Pray Together

My dear friend Jean told me, "Sometimes I have wanted to pray with a friend when we've talked about a problem, but I don't always like to be the one to take the initiative. And yet I would appreciate it so much if she would suggest it." I see an analogy between making love with your husband and praying with a best friend. Both can be deeply spiritual experiences, bonding you in a threefold cord with God.

And I understand Jean's wish that her friend share in taking the initiative to pray, just as I understand the desire of husbands for their wives occasionally to initiate lovemaking. I also realize that both lovemaking and prayer can be mishandled. They can be approached perfunctorily, outside of an atmosphere of deep caring or expectancy of God's involvement: the form without the power.

In Akron I had a friend named Carole who used to breathe deeply before we would pray together, and I knew she was stilling her heart before the Creator of the universe. She drove my thoughts to Him. Likewise, my friend Jean enters into prayer with so much caring for me that I feel deeply moved—toward her and toward God. She also has an attitude of expectancy, evidenced by the fact that she inquires a few days later, "How has God been answering our prayer?"

What Is a Best Friend?

When I talked to women and asked them if they had a best friend, some would say, "I have two best friends," or, "I have three best friends." When I objected, saying that seemed to contradict the word *best,* they persisted. I came to realize that while *best friend* often does mean the friend you love the most, it can also mean a friend with whom you have a deep rapport and would consider a soul mate, a kindred spirit. There is a special bond that sets friends like these apart from the rest, and though they are very rare, you may be blessed with more than one. In fact, considering the feminine tendency toward dependency, it would be healthy to seek more than one soul mate and to give our closest friends freedom to do the same.

Since I have developed two "best" friendships in my town, I've found that I'm less demanding of each of these women and that having more than one special friend has been a fatal chop to the grasping weed that has choked the life out of best friendships in my past. How we need to loosen our hold on our best friends! We need to encourage them not only to run to God but also to develop friendships with others.

Ann, a woman from Milwaukee, said, "Sally and I are best friends, but that doesn't mean we're always together. We may not even sit together in a meeting. We each try to be open to other people whom the Lord may put across our paths."

Aristotle expressed the concept of soul mates when he said, "Friendship is a single soul living in two bodies." Bets said of her friendship with Beth:

> There is not another person in the world who knows the things about me that Beth knows. She knows me inside and out. It's

something spiritual, something in our souls—we are to each other
like second selves. And it's funny, but my daughter as a little girl
recognized our bond. Beth had been in Texas for three years, and
during that time Adrienne was born. When Beth returned, she
walked in the room and saw Adrienne for the first time. Beth
closed her eyes and uttered a low, "Oh!" and somehow Adrienne
seemed to know that she had a second mother in Beth, and loved
her immediately.

Studies show that men, in sharp contrast to women, are not likely to
be able to name a best friend. In her research, Lillian Rubin found that
men shrugged off her questions about best friends: "Best friends are for
kids." One man, piqued, said, "Only a woman would have so damn
many questions about friends and make it so important."[3]

How interesting, therefore, that the very best friends in Scripture are
two men! I suspect that David and Jonathan were rare right-brained
males. Let me build my case.

Both were extremely accurate marksmen (David with his slingshot,
Jonathan with his bow) and this, scientists now suspect, is one indica-
tion of a dominant right hemisphere.[4] (There's an interesting passage
in Judges 20:16 that tells of "seven hundred chosen men who were left-
handed, each of whom could sling a stone at a hair and not miss.")
David was a poet, a psalmist, a harpist—all gifts that we would attrib-
ute to the creative right hemisphere. And, as we will see, Jonathan was
certainly able to express his feelings, which is also a strength of the
right hemisphere.

Knit Together in Soul, Not in Body

Their friendship is unusual, surpassing even the friendships of most
women. Men have accused David and Jonathan of being homosexual.
But if that were so, then the Lord, who clearly defines homosexuality as
sin, couldn't have said what He did about David: "For David had done
what was right in the eyes of the LORD and had not failed to keep any of
the LORD's commands all the days of his life—except in the case of Uriah
the Hittite" (1 Kings 15:5). I believe the reason many men are uncomfortable with David and Jonathan is that they have never experienced
this kind of friendship, except perhaps with a woman with whom they
are also sexually one.

In an article in *Christianity Today* the point is made that many men cannot grasp the difference between a one-flesh relationship and a one-soul relationship, but there is a great difference.[5] In a one-soul relationship there is a union of minds, hearts, and spirits, but not a union of bodies. The *King James Version* eloquently translates the "one in spirit" concept. It says the soul of Jonathan was knit with the soul of David (1 Sam. 18:1).

This Hebrew word translated "knit" is the very same word that is used to describe the intense love that Jacob had for his youngest son, Benjamin (Gen. 44:30). We are told that if any mischief came upon Benjamin, it would send Jacob to the grave in sorrow because his soul was knit with the soul of Benjamin. If we have been blessed with a good relationship with our parents or our children, we understand this. We feel their pain or joy as if it were our own. We are knit together, but not sexually.

Women say to me, "I long for the kind of soul mate you are describing—but how do I find her?" I am absolutely convinced that you cannot turn a friend into a soul mate, for soul mates are special gifts from God. I do believe God is more apt to give you what you long for if He is first in your life. If He is not, He may be protecting you from relational idolatry and wisely refusing you a best friend.

Whenever Steve and I moved, I've always had to wait patiently for a friendship—and that was a time when I really would flee to God. Looking back, I see that may have been His plan all along. But if He sees He is first, and if we are married, our husbands second, then He may trust us with a soul mate. Ask Him to open your eyes to someone with whom you can have a healthy friendship—a David and Jonathan friendship—one where you help one another find strength in God. Ask God for one or (this is probably healthier) a few soul mates. Then be alert, for God may place her right across your path.

The Greeting Scene

After listening to David for just a short time, Jonathan recognizes a kindred spirit. Amazingly, he then commits his life to David. I am reminded of the commitment Ruth made to Naomi. The distinguishing difference is that Ruth and Naomi had known each other for ten years, but David and Jonathan had just met.

> After David had finished talking with Saul, Jonathan became one
> in spirit with David, and he loved him as himself. From that day
> Saul kept David with him and did not let him return to his father's
> house. And Jonathan made a covenant with David because he
> loved him as himself. (1 Sam. 18:1–3)

Although Jonathan's choice of David as a best friend seems rather
abrupt, it was a very wise choice. We will be blessed if we seek best
friends with David's qualities.

Being Drawn to Saints and Poets

What drew Jonathan to David? As Jonathan listened to David converse
with his father, he must have recognized the poet—the psalmist—in
David. And as this right-brained male recognized a kindred spirit, his
soul was knit with the soul of David.

I played the role of Emily in our high school's presentation of *Our
Town*. One scene lingers in my memory. After Emily has died, she is
allowed to watch her loved ones on earth. She is poignantly aware that
they are scurrying about, taking life for granted, just as she did. With
tears in her eyes, Emily watches her mama and remembers the little
things, like "sunflowers, coffee, new-ironed dresses, and hot baths." She
cries, "Oh, earth, you're too wonderful for anybody to realize you." Then
she turns and asks the stage manager, "Do any human beings ever realize life while they live it?—every, every minute?"

And he answers, "No. The saints and poets, maybe—they do, some."[6]

Poets and saints see things other people miss. Luci Shaw takes a fast
mile walk along country roads every morning, and when she comes
home, she often sits down and writes the metaphors that God has
helped her to see. Luci is alert for "pictures in her head." She believes
God has opened her inner eyes and He speaks through her imagination.

When I am with Luci, I find that I start seeing things that I
couldn't before. Her vision flows into me a little, and it's as though
Jesus has put His healing hands on my sightless eyes and helped me
to see a little better.

Genuine poets are rare. But if we look carefully, most of us can find
people who have poets' imaginations, who stretch us because their
thoughts and their lifestyles have not been squeezed into the world's
mold. We can also find "saints" who are so abiding in Christ and His

Word that they see life differently from most Christians. Jesus says the mouth speaks what the heart is full of—and when you are with some people it is like sitting under a spiritual fountain, for you are continually being sprinkled with the overflow of a rich heart.

Poets are reflective, really *looking* at life and seeing—they ask thoughtful questions, drawing you out because they really care about how you think and feel. They take the road less traveled: They may be living simply, reading the classics, or dedicated to prayer. Poets embrace life! When I walk with my friend Shell, she'll suddenly stop and say, "Oh—look at the gossamer wings on that bug!" When I invite Lorinda over, she *savors* the split pea soup I've made. When I'm with Patti, she laughs out loud at the dog's thumping tail. My friend Janet is standing on my deck right now, "mesmerized" by the pale pink of the sky. They notice the simple gifts of God that so many miss.

Marla said of her soul mate: "I think she's my best friend because she stimulates me to think." A best friendship with a thinking person can be a catalyst in your life, helping you to reach beyond that which you've known before.

Being Drawn to Giant Slayers

There's another important clue illuminating the instant bonding between Jonathan and David. It appears two verses before this famous greeting scene. "As soon as David returned from killing the Philistine, Abner took him and brought him before Saul, with David still holding the Philistine's head" (1 Sam. 17:57). Picture this: David is holding the bloody and glassy-eyed head of Goliath when Jonathan first meets him. A gory but significant detail. It helps me to understand Jonathan's bonding to David, for I, too, am drawn to those who slay giants who have defied God.

Mindy said, "I am drawn to a person whom I would like to be like— I see that she has some quality that I would like to have." I believe we are drawn to giant slayers because they do what we long to do but sometimes are afraid to do.

My young friend Phyllis is a giant slayer. As David was angry about Goliath, Phyllis is angry about the giant, pornography. She speaks to women, showing them how pornography has contributed, significantly, to violent sexual crimes against women and children. Recently Phyllis was grocery shopping with her children and noticed that her store had begun carrying *Playboy* magazine and X-rated videos. She asked, politely, if she might see the store's manager. When he came out, she warmly extended her hand and introduced herself and her three wide-eyed children. "What may I do for you, ma'am?" he asked.

"I have liked shopping here," Phyllis began. "I appreciate your cleanliness, your good service, and your fair prices—but I've noticed that you are now carrying pornographic magazines and X-rated videos. Do you think this kind of material is appropriate in your family-centered store?"

The manager removed all of the unsavory material from his store. I am drawn to Phyllis as she stands there holding a giant's head.

Giant slayers seem to have better spiritual vision than other Christians. Perhaps this is because obedience, which is the essence of giant slaying, breeds deeper vision. It makes sense that God would trust those who obey with more of His wisdom. Why waste it on those who aren't going to apply it?

I look for giant slayers on the front lines: I notice the woman who is willing to take charge of Vacation Bible School or has adopted a retarded child. I would expect to find a few giant slayers praying for their children with a group like Moms in Touch, volunteering at a Crisis Pregnancy Center, or building homes with Habitat for Humanity. I know this: Giant slayers won't be sitting back with fear or apathy as giants defame God's name.

Recently a bright and enthusiastic speaker at a workshop at one of my retreats came up to me and said, "I want to tell you I read *The Friendships of Women* fifteen years ago and it changed my life. Not only was I delivered from homosexuality—but there were so many other things in that book that impacted me. Dee—I remember *so many things*." And then, bless her, she was *specific*, listing them, including, "I look for poets and giant slayers. I do! And it's made my friendships so rich."

Becoming Alert to Friends Who Will Help Us Grow

A best friendship begins, often, with the same sort of feelings that lovers feel when meeting. We notice something and are pulled. It may be giant slaying, it may be poetic vision, or it may be something ineffable, but we are drawn.

We would be wise to consider what attracts us to a woman. When we

are pulled to that which is lovely and Christlike, when we notice someone who is living a radically obedient life, then those are the best
impulses to act on. This is when it is definitely worth taking a risk in
reaching out to someone. For we will become like our closest friends.

One of the costliest mistakes we can make is to have a weak Christian
for a *best* friend. Paul has some grave warnings in 1 Corinthians 5:11
about choosing a close friend who calls himself a brother (or a sister) and
yet is sexually immoral, greedy, an idolater, or a slanderer. Does your best
friend feel she was born to shop? Does she cut others down with gossip?
Soon you will be like her. She won't drive you to God; she will drive you
to sin.

This does not mean we should not befriend non-Christians, and Paul
makes this clear in the same passage (see 1 Cor. 5:9–10). Indeed, we
have a responsibility to move beyond our Christian cloister and truly
love the lost into the kingdom. (Research shows that most adults who
came to Christ did so through the influence of a genuine friend. It also
shows, sadly, that most Christians are not truly befriending non-
Christians.[7]) By stating that our best friends should be strong
Christians, I am in no way negating our responsibility to become genuine
friends with non-Christians.

When your closest friends are strong in the Lord, it impacts you pro-
foundly. When I look at the really good choices I made this week, so
often they were influenced by a friend. Look, for example, at the last
few days:

> Friday: Traveling, stayed with Scharfs. Love the way they always
> read a psalm at breakfast and pray for a different country each day.
> I am reminded to be a world Christian, praying for countries. Their
> daughter-in-law talks about a book she has loved, *Girl Meets God*. I
> make a note to get it.
>
> Saturday: Walk with my friend Beth and we pray for our kids.
> We have a good discussion on how better to speak the truth in love.
> She tells me I must read the new boundaries book—*Face to Face:
> Having That Difficult Conversation*. I order it from Barnes and Noble.
> Amazing. Now I'm giving it to others.
>
> Sunday: Have lunch after church with Christy and Ellen. I tell
> them I've gained fifteen pounds since Steve's death—I'm turning to
> the false god of food for comfort, and I can't seem to stop. They
> pray for me on the spot. Then Ellen tells me about a free Bible study

on a Web site called *SettingCaptivesFree.com*. There's one specifically for food called *The Lord's Table*. It helped her—she think it will help me. I check it out—am starting it—excited about it.

My life is so much richer because the Lord has taught me to pray and look for certain kinds of friends for my closest friends.

Be Alert to Be Amazed

Friends like Ruth and Jonathan are gifts from God. Though we can't demand a gift, we can ask. James tells us we have not because we ask not.

Then, be alert to how God might be leading. I realize now that there were times God may have brought someone across my path, but I didn't recognize her because I had my own preconceived idea of what she would be like. I didn't think I'd be friends with Rebecca—she looked like my stereotype of a homeschooling mom. (Don't misunderstand—I'm all for homeschooling, but there are a lot of homeschoolers that seem a bit bound up in rules and dress.) But when I got to know Rebecca—wow, what a heart. She is one of the best listeners I've ever met—repeating back to you, days later, what you said. She is a reader of John Piper, R. C. Sproul, and Oswald Chambers. Being with her drives me to God. It would have been easy to miss Rebecca.

I have also learned that there are seasons when God wants me to walk alone. He knows my needs better than I do—and sometimes He knows we need to let Him be the Friend who is closer than a brother. This was the first summer since Steve's death and I "over-invited" people to my cabin, I was so fearful of being alone. I love everybody I invited, but I realize now that I need time alone with the Lord to fully grieve.

It is also possible to run ahead of Him and develop friendships that are good, but not the best. When we wait on Him, listening to Him, He may very well give us the gift of a friend of *His* choosing.

Our hearts, especially as women, long for kindred spirits. We also long, according to Proverbs 22:7, for unfailing love. Yet Solomon also tells us that these kinds of friends are very rare. If God gives us one special friend, we should cherish her and nurture her the way we would a rare rose.

CHAPTER NINE

UNFAILING LOVE

Hold a true friend with both hands.

—NIGERIAN PROVERB

When I was ten, I locked my sister's prom date in the fruit cellar. I thought it a tremendous joke as I watched her steam increase over his tardiness. But though she may have wanted to, Sally didn't disown me. She's my sister, and blood ties rarely end.

My adolescent passage was torment for the family confined to my shelter. Mother said it was like living with someone who was going through three nonstop years of premenstrual tension: If she raised an eyebrow, it could release hysteria from me. But she held on and waited for this time to pass. She's my mother, and blood ties rarely end.

My sisters and I live in three different states: Texas, Utah, and Nebraska. We have not been geographically close since we left our childhood home. But we see each other at least annually, and we stay in touch almost daily by e-mail. We are not going to allow the mobility of our lives to keep us from being close. We are sisters, and blood ties rarely end.

Blood Is Thicker Than Water

Writer Lesley Dormen said that her family isn't going to cross her off their Christmas card list if she is impatient or crabby. She elaborates:

> If my mother and I exchange hurtful words, the incident has the
> power to pierce both of us to the heart. But I know with absolute

certainty that neither my mother nor my brother will ever abandon me. We're bound to each other for good. We're family.... If I
have a falling-out with a friend, I can't just assume that the
breach will heal itself. A small fissure in a friendship has a way of
leading to permanent rupture unless both parties take special care
to mend it.[1]

Wistfully, Karen said, "Even though I may care very deeply for a
friend, and she for me—after a move, the friendship is pretty much in
the past. I'm not a very good correspondent."

Family ties seem to be stronger than friendship ties. In the case of
best friends, this realization can breed anxiety. Lillian Rubin says,
"There is a particular urgency between best friends that seems to seek
constant reassurance ... perhaps because of the experience of all the
friends who have passed through our lives and are long gone."[2]

Our longing for our friends to be like family is not for all friends—
but for a special few. It is important to understand the difference
between "annuals and perennials."

Annual and Perennial Friends

Think about the differing types of flowers. There are annuals—the
lovely but fragile petunias, pansies, and impatiens we put in our flower
boxes, knowing they will brighten our lives for just a season. But then
there are the hardy perennials—irises, tulips, or daisies that your grand-
mother may have planted and are still coming up faithfully each new
spring. Most friends are like annual flowers, but annual flowers are valuable. They can be there during those times when perennials are not at
their peak, adding color, variety, and beauty to our lives. For a season
they bless you (or you them), but then they fade away and are gone,
and even that is a blessing, for then there is room in your garden for
new and different annuals!

But now and then God gives you a perennial—a friend who comes
back season after season. You can't turn an annual into a perennial—a
perennial is simply a gift from God. They are the "Ruths" and the
"Jonathans" that God sends into your life to encourage you, to love
you, and to stand by your side with unfailing love.

Both perennials and family tend toward permanency—but perennials are often able to bless in ways that family may not.

Friends Can Be Sweeter Than Family

There are barriers to be overcome in sibling relationships. Mom really might have liked her better. Or we may have been frequently compared to a prettier, smarter, more popular sister. My sisters were both high-school homecoming queens, and I wasn't. Sally was only a sophomore when she was crowned queen, and my parents were so proud. I remember their glowing faces at the crowning! Three years later, their second daughter, Bonnie, was homecoming queen. I, the third daughter, never even made the court.

My parents tried to make me feel valuable ("You're the best water skier!") and tried not to show favoritism. But still, I felt I did not measure up to my popular sisters. And though no one may be at fault, memories like this can make it difficult to rejoice with an adult sister when she is promoted to an executive position or to weep with her when she gains ten pounds. Kathleen, a striking brunette, told me intently:

> I have two sisters who are very, very precious to me. But friends are different because you don't take a friend back to childhood with all of those old sibling rivalries that, no matter how old you are, are still there when you get to be a grown-up. There's an advantage to that because sometimes, when you are having a problem, your family will kind of sit back and empathize and help you on the outside, but inside they're thinking, GOOD!

There are barriers of birth order to be overcome as well. Tammy, the oldest in a family of four, said of her sisters, "I don't see them as my friends. I see them as people I'm responsible for."[3] Middle sisters often feel resentful of both the older and younger sisters as they had to compete for the attention over the firstborn and the baby. Younger sisters complain that they never are taken seriously. Katie said, "I wish my sister would stop treating me like a little sister. She sees my Christian beliefs as just another phase I'm going through—one thing that will pass in time."[4]

Maturity and Christ's love can break down these barriers. My sisters are now two of my very best friends. It isn't just that they're turning gray ahead of me—I am knit to them. When they hurt, I hurt. When they are full of joy, I am full of joy. But coming to this point of sisterly friendship took time and prayer. It isn't that way with friends. You start fresh. No memories of childhood quarrels. No parental favoritism. No sibling rivalry.

Friends Are Chosen

You can't choose your family. Sometimes we wish we could! But friends *are* chosen, and that gives them a special honor. However, if they can be chosen, then we realize they can be "unchosen." Perennial friendships *can* die. Though they are hardier than annual friendships, they are still vulnerable to enemies who destroy. Just as those hungry deer pawed through the snow and frozen earth to eat the tulip bulbs we'd planted at my husband's grave, perennial friendships may be destroyed through the enemies of betrayal or neglect.

Perennial Friends Call for Unfailing Love

Perennial friendships are so rare and precious—they call for unfailing love, or, in Hebrew, *hesed*. Solomon says that we each yearn for *hesed:* "What a man desires is unfailing love" (Prov. 19:22). This word expresses one of the most beautiful concepts in Scripture. It is also a thread that weaves its way through the generations of friendship we are examining.

There are two main thoughts intertwined in this complex Hebrew word. The first is that of mercy or kindness. The second is faithfulness. We want God's mercy, and we want it to keep on coming! The whole idea is perhaps expressed best in Lamentations 3:22–23: "Because of the LORD's great love we are not consumed, for his compassions never fail. They are new every morning; great is your faithfulness."

In their parting scene, Naomi prayed the Lord would show Ruth and Orpah *hesed* (translated "kindness" in most translations in Ruth 1:8). And when Ruth comes home from the field of Boaz with her arms full of grain, Naomi recognizes the answer to her prayer. She exclaims that the Lord has not stopped showing his kindness (*hesed*) to the living and the dead. (See Ruth 2:20.)

Hesed is what we yearn for from the Lord and from one another. We want our friends to be kind to us and never to abandon us. We want the kindness of friends intertwined with the permanence of family.

Chris, a woman in her late thirties, said, "I told my friend that I had always wanted a sister, and it was a little late for my mother to adopt.

She laughed and said, 'If it will make you feel any better, I'll adopt you. I'll be your sister.'" In making our friends like family, we are saying, "I may let you down, I may move away—but please, don't let that end our bond. Let's be as permanent as family." This unfailing love is *hesed.* Christ embodies *hesed,* and as we embody Christ, our best friendships should never end.

Jonathan promised *hesed* to David in their greeting scene, and then later requested it of David when he said, "Show me unfailing kindness [*hesed*] like that of the LORD as long as I live" (1 Sam. 20:14). And David made a covenant with Jonathan, promising him unfailing love. This passage becomes even more moving when you realize that it was the custom when a new king came to power for the old king's family to be murdered.

Though Jonathan was next in line for the throne, he felt that David was God's man. In supporting David, he was endangering not only his own life but also the lives of his future children. So he asks David for an oath of unfailing love, "so that I may not be killed." And he adds, "And do not ever cut off your kindness from my family" (1 Sam. 20:15).

The recognition that they were committed to this friendship is what made David and Jonathan like brothers. In fact, *The Living Bible* has David saying to Jonathan, "Do this for me as my sworn brother" (1 Sam. 20:8).

Should We Make a Friendship Vow?

Both Jonathan and Ruth made a friendship promise to their soul mates. In the original edition of *The Friendships of Women* I suggested being open to making friendship promises with soul mates one had known a long time. However, I no longer advise it as a practice. Yes, it happened with Ruth and Naomi and also with David and Jonathan—but all of these friends were facing exceptional circumstances, which is what I failed to take into account. Naomi had lost her whole family and was devastated. Ruth's vow was given, not to bind Naomi to her, but to show Naomi that she was determined to be faithful to her, even in the most difficult circumstances.

Likewise, the threat of death was clearly over both David and Jonathan, and they needed to know the other would be there for them in their time of need. Would God ever lead us to make a vow? It is possible, in extremely rare circumstances. I promised my dear young friend Rita, who was twenty-three and dying, that I would be her friend and find a wife for her husband and a mother for her children. She pleaded with me, I promised, and God allowed me to fulfill my vow beautifully. But that kind of scenario is extremely rare. I have learned that it is better to be content with an implicit vow than to make a verbal vow before God. Let me explain.

After my original edition of *The Friendships of Women* was released, I received some alarming mail and phone calls. One mother wrote me that her daughter read my book as a freshman at college and then made a lifelong friendship vow to her counselor, with whom she had been meeting for just one month! Another mother called me because she feared her daughter was getting into an unhealthy friendship with an older woman. This woman was discipling her and had asked her, on the basis of my book, to move in with her and make a promise of unfailing love to her. Whoa! Red flags waved at me.

Both of the above examples shout to me, "relational idolatry!" Asking someone to bind herself to you with a vow after a short period of time sounds very unhealthy. Though it is true David and Jonathan vowed friendship shortly after they met, they were in life and death circumstances. If someone is pressuring you to make a vow quickly, whether it is for friendship or for marriage—don't! Pressure comes from the father of lies—not the Holy Spirit. The enemy doesn't want us to slow down, think, pray, or wait on the Lord. Pressure to hurry and make a decision is one of his most common tricks. Don't fall for it.

It is also *very* serious to make a vow before God. In Ecclesiastes 5:2–6 we are told to be very cautious about making a vow, for God expects you to keep it and He *will* destroy the work of your hands if you break your vow.

Does God ever lead a person to make a verbal vow? Yes. In the case of marriage, God's Word is clear that He wants you to be true until death. In that case, a verbal vow *does not add* to what God has already required of you, but is a reminder of that requirement. My friend Jan Silvious has explained to me that the word friendship comes from a root word meaning "free." One of the beautiful things about friendship is that it is free. God does not require us to maintain all friendships forever.

It is not unusual for God to bring a very dear friend into your life for a season. When that season is passed, He may allow you to drift apart, though you may always feel a love for that person. But if you have vowed lifelong love to that friend, then you are bound to her, even though God might have loosed you! Sometimes it is hard for us to know, in our limited vision, if a friend is an annual or a perennial.

However, having said that, there comes a time in a perennial friendship when being untrue will feel like betrayal, and, in fact, is. For both of you are aware of an "implicit" vow.

Implicit Bonds

In *King Lear,* Cordelia will not promise her father unfailing love as her sisters do, because she says there is an unspoken bond between them. And interestingly, only Cordelia remains true to her father. Shakespeare is teaching us that vows are not only as good as the character of the person making them, but also some implicit bonds should remain strong without vows.

Bets and Beth, best friends, have not spoken vows to each other, but each is aware of an implicit bond. Bets said, "I know, I am absolutely convinced, that if I *ever* need Beth, she'll be there for me. We don't need to promise it." And Beth agrees: "I am in this friendship for the long haul—no matter what."

Author Walter Wangerin says that vows don't have to be spoken in order for there to be a covenant between two people. He explains that every communal relationship is modeled on the primary relationship (God and man) and so has covenant in it. The covenant or code "is mostly unspoken, but both partners know it; and as long as both obey it, the relationship is protected and nourished as a living thing."[5]

When a close friend breaks that unspoken covenant by sharing your secrets, neglecting you in a time of great need, or committing another treachery, it hurts because it should. There has indeed been a trampling of life. Wangerin seems to understand. He writes of a woman who has been betrayed. The friend that she had trusted so and felt such life with and had revealed the whole of her soul to—naked and unashamed—has told others. Today the betrayed one sits in her apartment and can't stop crying, can't stop feeling angry with herself for being so trusting. Wangerin writes:

> I put my arm around you ... I tell you the sad news: that you may not be able to sleep tonight; that tomorrow the whole world might seem alien and strange to you; that in the weeks to come you might not be able to concentrate on the simplest tasks of your job, and you might let your apartment get messy, and you may sink into a mindless depression. But immediately I tell you the kinder news: this is all normal. Don't think something like a poor diet or crummy weather caused your sorrow. Dear, you've suffered a significant death. The very arteries of your communal life were cut asunder. Trust was destroyed by her that was your friend, and lifeblood ran from the wound. You have a right to grieve.[6]

Forgiveness and grace may bring healing, but it will take time for these significant wounds to heal and for life to be restored. Let us acknowledge that implicit vows are indeed vows and should be treated with the care of unfailing love.

Twenty-two years ago Lee and I bonded when the Lord used me as a vessel to bring Lee to Christ. Though we've been separated geographically for twenty years, we've nurtured our friendship through letters and e-mail.

Lee has come to hear me speak many times. Many years ago, when I had not yet seen the danger of making friendship vows, she heard me suggest, when speaking in New York, the possibility of considering a friendship vow. That night Lee told me, earnestly, "I can't make a promise, because I'm so afraid I would break it." I respected Lee's hesitancy, for it sprang out of a healthy fear of the Lord. I appreciate it all the more now.

I am also confident of our implicit bond and our unspoken commitment to nurture it. As Lee and I rode in the airport bus to catch our separate planes, we felt the bittersweet pain of parting. Lee caught my hands in hers and said, "We are knit together, my friend. As Jonathan was knit to David, so I am knit to you."

Each of us needs to assess our implicit bonds. There are those who are going to feel rightfully let down if we fail them, even though no blood ties exist and no promises have been made. Leisa said, "I know I've got to get over it, but I was absolutely shocked when my best friend since kindergarten didn't come to my wedding." There was an implicit bond there that was not honored.

There may very well be a time under heaven to close the door on friendships, especially the loose ties. Each of us can maintain only a limited number of close ties. But I believe we too easily are closing doors on the "real connections," and falling into the world's mold of impermanence and easy good-byes when we fail to be true to the people whose souls have been knit with ours.

Twenty-five years ago I did something that has been enormously helpful to me. I went to a solitary place and met with the Lord, asking Him: "Lord, to whom do You want me to be true?" Because Steve and I moved frequently during our marriage, we made many long-distance friends whom we love; and yet I cannot be true to all of them. (There are only so many people to whom I can give unfailing love at any given time.) And so I asked God to impress on my heart the names of the long-distance friends to whom He wanted me to be true.

Some of the questions I asked were: "Am I knit to her?" "Has she shown a desire to be faithful to me?" "How are You leading, Lord?" God impressed on my heart the names of four long-distance friends. It's rewarding to look back over these twenty-five years and see that I have been fairly true to those four women! (I say "fairly" because I have feet of clay—but Jesus truly has been helping me.) To none of them have I made a verbal vow, yet God showed me we have an implicit vow. E-mail is such a painless and unobtrusive way to stay in touch. If you haven't learned how to use it, get help and discover how easy it is. You'll wonder how you lived without it. I can also put on a headset and call from my cell phone when I'm driving or doing dishes.

I knew I needed to be at Lee's daughter's wedding, to fly to see Lorinda when she was battling cancer, and to pray Patti through her husband's long illness. There is life in those friendships, life I do not want to fail to nourish; and I saw that life flow back to me when Steve was so sick, and now when I have to live without him.

The model we have in the New Testament is continued prayer, letter writing, and if possible, occasional visits to those who have been our cherished friends. With e-mail, short letters are easy. Use the perennial calendar on your computer to remind you of a friend's birthday. It's great to be reminded each year with a little box appearing, saying, "Patti's birthday is coming up!"

When Jan moved from Scottsbluff, Nebraska, halfway across the state to Kearney, she pined for Nancy, the soul mate she'd left behind.

Jan showed me a picture of Nancy and her husband hanging on her wall like the picture of a treasured family member. She also showed me the figures of two little straw girls hugging each other that Nancy had recently sent to her. "Not a week goes by when we don't write or call. This is a permanent friendship."

For friends nearby, bonds can be maintained with lunch dates, phone calls, and short notes of love. Unfailing love means anticipating a friend's needs and following up on her concerns. My friend Carol will make a brief phone call to check on me. My neighbor Jo told me that she lay awake one night thinking of a title for this book, a concern she knew had been on my heart. Charlotte put it like this: "They're paying attention."

We need to assess our real connections and then remain true. Ruth, a fifty-eight-year-old nurse, said, "A good, warm friendship, like a good, warm fire, needs continual stoking."

Basing Relationships on Commitment

When Steve and I were starry-eyed newlyweds, we were convinced that our marriage would remain strong on love alone. One of our first "couple" friendships was with Dan and Lorinda, a darkly handsome couple who knew how to live life with passion on a shoestring! They'd refurbished an old home on top of Queen Anne Hill in Seattle. They lived romantically—with candles, classical music, and love well laced with laughter.

One evening after supper, as we were lingering over coffee and fresh raspberry pie, Dan began talking about the glue of his marriage. He surprised us by saying that his marriage to Lorinda was going to last because of commitment, not love. (*How unromantic!* we thought.) He said his feelings for Lorinda might rise and fall (*Lovely Lorinda?* we questioned) but that his commitment to her would be steadfast.

As the years passed, we came to see the wisdom of Dan's words. And just as marriages need to be based on commitment rather than feelings, so do cherished friendships. Sooner or later we will all reveal our feet of clay.

And women, probably more than men, tend to have their feelings hurt. Our hides are tender, and the very fact that we are closer and value friendship so much makes us correspondingly more vulnerable.

Mary told me about how her best friendship ended:

> I was pregnant and I wasn't ready to tell anyone—not even
> Annie. She suspected and asked me, and I lied. It was wrong; I'm
> sorry I did it—but I did. She felt so betrayed when she found out
> the truth that she never really could find it in her heart to forgive
> me. We tried to mend things, but it was never the same. And
> then, when she moved away, she didn't write. Ever. And when
> she came back to visit, she didn't come to see me. I felt rejected.
> We were so close—and we were sisters in Christ! I wish she would
> forgive me.

If Annie's friendship with Mary had been based on commitment
rather than feelings, I believe the friendship would have been salvaged.
There still would have been a period when Annie would not have felt
the same love for Mary that she had once, but I believe God would have
restored those feelings. A huge part of *hesed* is mercy or grace. We must
understand that we are all sinners, so, sooner or later, we *are* going to
let each other down. We need to be merciful to one another. We need
to give one another grace.

Amazing Grace

Grace isn't natural, but supernatural. The natural responses when you
get hurt are either to strike back or to withdraw. When we instead step
out of the way and allow God to work through us, responding with
unfailing love, even perennials that have endured a deep freeze may lift
up their wilting heads and live.

In the midst of the original writing of this chapter, my soul mate,
Shell, and I had a "freeze." I am knit to Shell and she is the one friend
to whom I have made a verbal vow (when I thought that was what
Scripture modeled). Shortly after I vowed friendship to her, we had an
awful argument! Mothers can become like mother bears when they are
discussing "the right way" to raise children, and we both snarled,
roared, and bared our teeth. I had always thought Shell was far too strict
as a mother.

I thought, *Why, Shell's girls aren't allowed to do anything!* She
thought I was far too lenient. She thought, *Doesn't Dee know that
boundaries are important in raising children?* (Today, twenty-five years
later, we realize that God *gave* us each other, in part, to temper the

other. We call ourselves "law" and "grace." Our daughters, now nearly thirty years old, are women who love the Lord fervently.)

Shell reflected recently, smiling, "Obviously all the credit goes to God, for we sure did it differently!" That terrible day of our argument, neither one of us was slow to speak, quick to listen, or slow to become angry. Shell left my house in tears.

I went to my husband, Steve, hoping for empathy, telling him of my hurt. Steve gently said, "I wonder if God is testing you."

"What do you mean?"

"Well, here you are in the midst of writing a book about the friendships of women. Now you have had a quarrel with a very dear friend. It seems this could be a test—an opportunity to live what you are teaching."

I was silent. I didn't like where this was going. But I also realized Steve really could be right. If he was, then I had better pass the test. I confess I sought God out at that point, not because of conviction, but because I was afraid that if I didn't He wouldn't bless the book I was writing. The sinner does not easily turn, but God, in His mercy, can turn the sinner. And that's what He did—for when I was still before Him, He showed me my pride, my cruelty, and my insensitivity.

I picked up the phone and called Shell. When she answered, I told her I was truly sorry. She was quiet, but then she thanked me for calling.

I thought our friendship would quickly resume—but she stopped coming over, stopped calling.

So, I went back to Steve. Surely *now* he would give me empathy!

"I told Shell I was sorry. But she's freezing me out."

He put his arm around me. Encouraged, I said, "I don't think she realizes what a precious friend she might be losing in me." At that, Steve laughed!

Then he said, "I've heard *you* say that sometimes saying you are sorry isn't enough. Sometimes that can be remorse rather than repentance. You've said that sometimes you have to bear the fruit of repentance to convince the one you have wronged that you are truly sorry."

Again, I was silent. But, again, I tried. I wrote Shell a note telling her some of the reasons I loved her. When I *still* didn't hear from her, I baked her blueberry muffins as an excuse to go to her house.

When she opened the door, we fell into each other's arms, weeping. She said, "Dee, I was going to forgive you—just not so quickly." We both laughed.

In our case, God restored our friendship. But what do you do if a friend does not respond to your sincere apology and acts of love?

When an Angry Friend Doesn't Respond

After trying repeatedly to restore one friendship with words of apology, gifts, and notes, I realized that every attempt I'd made had intensified my friend's anger. I went to my sister Sally for advice. She suspected it was an attack from Satan. I was so drained of energy and concentration from my futile attempts at trying to restore this broken relationship that I listened carefully when my sister said:

> Lay it down before the Lord, Dee. You've done what you can to be
> at peace with her. When she comes to mind, you can pray for her
> and for healing, but lay it down and trust God's sovereignty.

In most cases, unfailing love, given sincerely, will restore a broken relationship—but if it doesn't, then my sister's advice is wise. If you've tried to restore the friendship with the same gentleness and skill that a cardiovascular surgeon uses when performing open-heart surgery, and you intuitively sense that the "patient" (your friendship) is getting worse, then stop! Don't plunge the knife in out of frustration or anger, but stop the surgery, sew it up, and take your hands off. Leave your friend prayerfully in God's hands and trust His sovereignty. Joseph had to do this when his brothers hated him, and eventually God brought good out of a very painful situation. (See Gen. 45:1–8.)

In some cases, restoration may not take place. You may be dealing with an unbeliever or a believer who isn't willing to forgive. But even in this, if we continually respond to evil with unfailing love, God will be glorified and we will be refined, like gold over the fire.

Unfailing Love Is Costly

If you choose to give someone unfailing love, be prepared to pay a price. There are going to be times when it seems easier to say good-bye—because you've been genuinely hurt, or because the friend is needing so much help, or because it simply takes discipline to keep up a long-distance friendship. But this is where Christians should be different from those who do not have the model and strength of Christ.

Jonathan asked David to show him "unfailing love like that of the Lord." And what is that like? It is love given at great personal cost. As Christ gave His life for us when we were betraying Him, so should we continue loving even when we are feeling betrayed.

Betrayal, according to a test administered by *Psychology Today* to 40,000 friends, is the main reason close friendships end.[7] Sooner or later one friend is going to reveal her feet of clay and commit an act of mild or severe betrayal. Sometimes, if we are prone to relational idolatry, we may interpret a withdrawal as a betrayal when it is not.

Marriage counselor Karen Huston told me that most intimate relationships, such as marriage and best friendships, have a natural rhythm of intense closeness and drifting apart. Since both of these conditions have a degree of inherent discomfort, we vacillate between the two: we're close, and then we feel the need for space; we're apart, and then we miss each other. If we interpret the natural drifting-apart period as betrayal (which it isn't), then out of hurt or anger we may become the betrayer.

In *The Best of Friends, the Worst of Enemies,* author Eva Margolies tells of how hurt Cara was when she wasn't seeing as much of her best friend, Irene.[8] Rather than continuing to give Irene unfailing love, Cara found an opportunity, when Irene's father died, to hurt Irene as she had been hurt. Cara decided, despite a tearful call from Irene, to skip the funeral. Irene was deeply wounded at a vulnerable time in her life—her acquaintances all came to the funeral, but her best friend was missing. Eventually, because of a confrontation from Irene, Cara and Irene were able to work out their differences. But so often in a situation like this, we simply let a cherished friendship die.

The most difficult time to give a friend unfailing love is when we're feeling as though they no longer care deeply for us. Our carnal nature desires to inflict pain, not extend kindness! And yet, when we give unfailing love to a person who doesn't seem to deserve it, that is when we are most like Christ.

At great peril to his own life, Jonathan demonstrated unfailing love by discovering his father's plan to murder David and warning his friend. Weeping because of the pain of parting, Jonathan nevertheless insists that David flee for his life.

The Parting Scene

In this most poignant of parting scenes, David is facedown before Jonathan, weeping with abandon. It is Jonathan who helps David to gain control by saying, "Go in peace, for we have sworn friendship with each other in the name of the LORD, saying, 'The LORD is witness between you and me, and between your descendants and my descendants forever'" (1 Sam. 20:42).

This scene reminds me of one Kathleen described concerning her move from Texas. As she and her best friend were having a good cry, Kathleen sobbed, "What will I do without you?"

Kathleen's friend gained control of herself and said, "You'll be fine." Kathleen said:

> I wanted to say, "How can you say that? I won't be fine! I'll be miserable!" But that was truly the best thing she could have said to me. If she had allowed herself to continue to be as morose and depressed as I was, then she couldn't have helped me. Instead she gave me strength. She was really truly being my friend.

And Jonathan was truly being David's friend, giving him strength and control with a reminder of their promise of unfailing love.

Jonathan was true to David until death. David was true to Jonathan as well, though he showed his fallibility in the long lapse before he remembered, for Jonathan's son Mephibosheth was a young man before David follows through. (The story is in 2 Samuel 9.) But in the end, David did follow through.

We long for unfailing love, and we can ask the Lord to help us show it and receive it. But we must also realize that we are all sinners, and despite the best of intentions, we are going to let each other down. Genuine friends are like roses—breathtakingly lovely and worth the pain of an occasional surprising jab from a hidden thorn.

There are people, however, who look like roses, but aren't roses at all. They are alligators. Can you tell the difference between a rose and an alligator?

Chapter Ten

ROSES AND ALLIGATORS

K risten Ingram recalls the following conversation with her grandson Andrew when he was almost three:

> "Gra'mother?"
> "Yes, Andrew?"
> "Gra'mother, a dog is a friend!"
> "Yes," I said, "a dog is a friend."
> There was a period of silence, and then ...
> "Gra'mother?"
> "Yes, Andrew?"
> "A cat is a friend!" he said.
> "Yes, Andrew," I agreed, "a cat is a friend."
> There was a much longer silence, and then ...
> "Gra'mother!"
> "Yes, Andrew?"
> "Gra'mother, I don't think an alligator is a friend," he said with
sad certainty.[1]

Most women are like roses. As roses vary from quiet pink to sunny yellow to razzmatazz red, so do women. And when you draw near to a woman, she will often quite willingly open to you petal after petal of fragrant loveliness.

But lurking beneath the glossy, green leaves of roses are surprisingly nasty thorns. After experiencing a few jabs into your soft, tender flesh, you handle roses with more respect. A dedicated rose gardener, one who believes that the glory of the rose more than compensates for the occasional wounds it inflicts, learns to bear the pain and to handle roses in such a way that she is seldom injured.

Don't Be Shocked by Betrayal

When a friend lets us down, we show that our theology is off base when we're overcome with shock. The Bible teaches that we're all going to let each other down. Even the most beautiful rose has thorns. Preaching professor at Trinity Evangelical Seminary, Greg Scharf, says, "When someone fails you, don't be stunned! It's more appropriate to think, *Hmmmm! That confirms what Scripture teaches—that we're all sinners, that there's none that is righteous, no, not one.*"

Hopefully you've realized the folly of putting your trust in people. It's a hard lesson to learn. Charlie Brown has to relearn it every fall when Luci convinces him to trust her and let her hold the football for him. Every autumn Charlie Brown falls flat on his back.

We need to mature to the point where we realize that, while it is important to love and cherish our friends, our dependence should be on God alone—for only He is without sin, and only He will never let us down.

It does hurt to be jabbed by a thorn, especially if we have tried to show that friend unfailing love and it seems unappreciated. But we need to learn to be as tolerant of others' failings as we are of our own. It's also vital to our spiritual health to forgive those jabs. We're to be tenderhearted and compassionate toward others, just as in Christ, God has been tenderhearted and forgiving toward us (Eph. 4:32). It also helps to realize that when a person does let us down, it is usually not intentional.

Don't Take Offenses Personally

When a rose gardener is jabbed by a thorn, she realizes the rose had no personal animosity toward her but was simply born with thorns. We'd be wise to see people that way.

Polly's friend Kim was incensed when Polly forgot to stop by after work as planned so that Kim could fit a dress she was making for Polly. On the phone, despite Polly's sincere apology, her friend said, "Obviously you don't respect the fact that my time is valuable!" Polly said:

> It wasn't that at all. I respect Kim immensely and I could kick myself that I forgot. It was especially bad because I kept her waiting for thirty minutes at a restaurant just last month. But neither incident was a result of my feelings for her. Both were due to the

fact that I'm juggling too many balls in my life and sometimes I drop one. Maybe you've got to be a single mother to understand that, but I still think she should have accepted my apology before she brought me to tears. She said, "Promise that it won't happen again." I couldn't even do that—because although you can be sure I'm going to try, I know I'm not perfect.

As women, we are quicker than men to assume that an injury is the result of a person's feelings toward us. One husband despaired:

Susie has been in a blue funk all week, simply because I mentioned the top of the refrigerator was dusty. She's too short to see the dust, so I pointed it out, but I certainly regret it! How do I make her realize that my comment had nothing to do with my feelings about her or about her worthiness as a homemaker?

Perhaps our sensitivity shows how little confidence we have in ourselves. Perhaps it is a negative side effect of our global brain functions. A man can zero in on a problem, but a woman has trouble separating a problem from her feelings. We could thicken our skin if we would realize that most hurts are not a reflection of the perpetrator's dislike for us, but rather a reflection of a hardship in the person's life, or a character flaw, or even a reflection of respect based on the assessment that we can handle criticism given in love.

Since I have grasped this principle, I'm more tolerant of friends who keep me waiting. I used to assume that their lack of punctuality was directly related to their feelings for me. While I was waiting, I stewed about that. Now I realize that people who are habitually late would keep the pope waiting!

Cover an Offense with Love

The most important time to appreciate the beauty of a rose is immediately following being stuck by a thorn. Writer Gini Kopecky said that she has a friend who thinks nothing of canceling long-term plans with her if something more attractive comes up. "It really insulted and infuriated me at first. So much so that at one point I seriously contemplated breaking off the friendship." But the more Gini thought about it, the more she realized that she didn't want to end the friendship.

There were too many things about this woman that I valued—her incredible energy, her sense of humor, her amazing kindness. I remember once she gave a party and right in the middle of it I got dizzy and almost fainted. And she was right there. She took me across the hall into a neighbor's empty apartment and sat with me until I had recovered. I'll never forget that. Now, I simply don't make long-term plans with this friend. I know what I can expect from our friendship, and I know what I can't. It's worth it to me not to demand from her what I know she can't give.[2]

Gini reflected on the things that she appreciated about her friend, and also reminded herself of a past evidence of her love. This is what 1 Peter 4:8 means when it says, "Love covers over a multitude of sins." Gini also wisely took a good look at the thorn (the canceling of long-term plans) and determined how to avoid being jabbed in the future. I've done this with a friend who cannot keep confidences. She's a dear friend and would do almost anything for me except keep my secrets. Because I treasure her and don't want to write her off as a friend, I am simply cautious about sharing any confidences with her that I wouldn't want spilled.

If I decide that I cannot cover a particular offense with love because the offense is too dismaying, then I have another scriptural alternative.

Confront with Love

Confrontation is tricky. It's painful and has ended many a friendship. We all have logs in our own eyes, so it seems a bit presumptuous to go after the speck in our sister's eye. Charlotte said, "I don't think we can go willy-nilly telling our friends that they would be all right if they would just take a little tuck here and a little tuck there!" I agree.

Yet Solomon tells us, "Better is open rebuke than hidden love" (Prov. 27:5) and, "Wounds from a friend can be trusted" (Prov. 27:6). So there is a time for confrontation, but it should pass a few tests.

Be sure your anger is healed. If your motivation is to hurt or to release your anger, then the situation will only get worse.

Pray, pray, pray—for your heart and for hers.

Don't prepare the sandwich approach (start with loving words, then *wham,* then end with loving words). Instead, speak the truth in love *all the way through.*

Plan to do it face-to-face if possible. If you must e-mail, write the letter in a document to attach to the e-mail (so you don't press "send" in haste) and sit on it for a few days.

Use "I" messages instead of the pointing "you" messages. For example, "I felt dishonored when our lunch date was forgotten. Help me understand why there was no apology."

Tell them what you want to see happen. "I don't mind when you borrow my iPod for your morning jog if you put it back where you found it."

Billie prayed about confronting her friend Rhonda for a long time and then prepared carefully. Billie tells the story:

> Rhonda led me to the Lord and I owed her my life! I also cherished her as a friend. She's terribly funny, yet serious about her walk with Christ. I truly loved her. But she was smothering me. If I wasn't with her, I felt like I had to give her an accounting. If I didn't have time to be with her, I could hear this hurt sound in her voice. I really didn't want to flee the friendship, but it couldn't go on like this.
>
> After praying about it, literally for weeks, I went to her and shared my feelings. I told her that I felt we were too dependent on each other and that the Lord was showing me, as a remedy, that it was time to develop other friendships. I also told her how much she meant to me and that I didn't want to lose her. To prove it, I asked her to go out to eat with me the next month on a specific date. It worked. We're still good friends and I'm much happier with the friendship.

Luci Shaw told me that confrontation is difficult for her because she is afraid that if she is outspoken and critical, she may lose the love and approval of the people who matter to her. But still, Luci is learning to speak truth in love. Recently, she mustered the courage to confront a treasured friend about a broken promise. "I felt for the sake of our friendship that I had to. She broke down, and we cried together. She felt that she had failed me, but we were closer after that because I had been honest. As hard as it was for both of us, it was worth it."

In both of these incidents, the women confronted in order to save the friendship. Our motivation for confrontation should always spring from a desire to improve the relationship or seek the other person's best. If we confront just to release anger, we destroy rather than build up.

I met Brooke—a career woman who could have passed for a *Vogue* model—on a flight to San Francisco. At first I felt intimidated by her sophisticated physical appearance and by the discovery that she had built up a thriving investment business in downtown Cleveland. But Brooke helped me over my sense of inferiority with warm and caring questions.

Soon we were talking about the friendships of women, and I was surprised to see tears in the eyes of this woman I'd judged as being invincible. Brooke's pain came from a confrontation that she had received from Ellen, a close friend since kindergarten, whose life had taken a different path from hers. "She has a lovely family—I adore her children. Perhaps all the more since I don't have a family of my own." Brooke told me the story:

> It was the afternoon after Ellen had picked me up at my office. She'd never been there before and it happened to be that crazy day when the stock market fell so many points. I had to handle a few long-distance calls and give several orders to employees before I could leave. Watching me, Ellen seemed impatient, strained … and her mood continued through lunch. I didn't know what was wrong, but later she called me and said, "I never want to see you in your place of work again. You can come to my home, or we can meet to shop. But I never want to see you there again."

I asked Brooke if she had probed Ellen for an explanation. She answered:

> A little, but frankly, I was afraid to. I'd already been dealt a staggering blow, and I wasn't sure I could take more. This incident has diminished both of us. Our friendship will suffer, for now I feel that when I'm with her I'm going to have to be a different person. My career is 95 percent of who I am, and she doesn't want to see that part of me.

Ellen didn't confront a specific behavior, but attacked the person and her whole identity. If we are attacking a whole person, it could be that Satan is on the prowl. Satan accuses, but there is not a specific behavior, just a general shame. The Holy Spirit convicts of a specific behavior that the person can repent of. Brooke could not "repent" of being a career woman.

Let us examine our hearts before we confront. We may feel threatened when a woman chooses to homeschool or not to homeschool because we have chosen the opposite path. But where is it written that one is right and one is wrong? The same is true in many areas. Gray areas are addressed in Romans 14, and we are told not to judge one another in gray areas but to be fully persuaded in our own minds about our own behavior. If *you* feel led not to wear slacks or to work part-time as a mother or to abstain from all wine, then that's what you should do. But don't judge your sister who has chosen another path. And don't feel that her choices are a judgment on you!

I remember getting an emotional call from a close friend who told me that she thought I didn't respect her—that I thought her life was less valuable because she was a stay-at-home mom who loved to cook from scratch. I was so surprised, for there was not a grain of truth in her thoughts. Instead, I often felt inadequate around her because she was such an amazing mom and hostess. I believe Satan was accusing my gifted and amazing friend, for that is his way. Yet I was so thankful for her call because it allowed me to affirm her and her choices. I was able to tell her how often I had seen her bless others (and me!) through her gift of hospitality, how beautifully her girls were turning out, and how certain I was that she was being true to God's calling of her and her wonderful gifts.

Part of the beauty of the body of Christ is that He does call different members to operate differently, yet we are one. (In the sequel to this book, *We Are Sisters,* I expand on this topic. I have seen how one of Satan's main techniques is to divide and scatter the sheep through lies and deception, and we must be on the offensive! We *are* sisters, and we must not let the enemy break up the fold.)

Sometimes a confrontation comes from insecurity or even a desire to hurt—but often it comes from being able to see our blind spots. Have you ever had the experience of almost pulling into another lane but then, at the last minute, seeing another car in your blind spot? Friends can help us see those blind spots, alert us to a car in our path, and help us swerve to safety.

Grow at the Hands of Your Critics

Whether the person's motive for confronting us is good or evil, we'd be wise to learn a lesson from Dawson Trotman, the founder of the Navigators. No matter how unfair the criticism might seem to be, he would prayerfully spread it before the Lord in his prayer closet and say, "Lord, please show me the kernel of truth hidden in this criticism."[3] One of the ways we can measure our maturity is by how we respond to confrontation. Solomon says:

> Do not rebuke a mocker or he will hate you; rebuke a wise man and he will love you. Instruct a wise man and he will be wiser still; teach a righteous man and he will add to his learning. (Prov. 9:8–9)

Alligators

The difference between a rose and an alligator is that a rose may never hurt you, but an alligator is likely to destroy you. Alligators demonstrate a *pattern of destruction*. Every rose has a few thorns, but an alligator is covered with them. His smile reveals jagged teeth lining his long snout. From the back of his neck to the muscled whip of his tail run rough, dangerous barbs. Your chances of escaping major injury if you cozy up to an alligator are slim.

Saul was an alligator. Repeatedly, he tried to pin David to the wall with his spear. When this failed, he sent David into battle with the Philistines, demanding one hundred Philistine foreskins for the hand of his daughter, Michal, in marriage. I imagine Saul thought David would die in battle, but the Lord was with him so he didn't.

Jonathan, in defense of his friend, tried to confront Saul. Saul seemed remorseful, as alligators sometimes are, and even took an oath of good behavior, but eventually he slipped into his destructive pattern again and tried to kill not only David but also Jonathan.

Some people believe that alligators are always of the female gender, but alligators come in either sex. Another extremely confusing thing is that many alligators claim to be believers. Saul certainly did, and often his words sound very spiritual. Yet if you look at the fruit in Saul's life, you can see his core was rotten. He may have been very "religious," but he demonstrated a complete lack of fear for God.

The thorns of an alligator, unlike the thorns of a rose, are life-threatening. Alligators put your spiritual, emotional, or physical life in jeopardy. Experts testify that three acts of violence in an abusive situation is evidence of a pattern. In the same way, if a "friend" has demonstrated a pattern of destruction, you would be wise to flee. Connie told me:

> I've worked as a secretary in four different offices. I'd never had

any serious problem with coworkers until Lorraine. Lorraine had been the executive secretary for fifteen years, and she had Mr. Johnston wrapped around her finger. I'd heard her discredit the other secretaries to him. She never failed to seize an opportunity to mention if someone had come in late, or misplaced a document, or whatever—half of the things she said just weren't true. One time, three other secretaries and I confronted her, together. She seemed surprised, even sorry. But then her viciousness became intense. She stabbed us in the back, one by one. The firings began and the women left with poor references. I hadn't been fired, but I wondered how long I'd be able to keep my job with Lorraine on the loose. When I felt Mr. Johnston's attitude toward me growing wary and cold, I suspected Lorraine. So before he fired me, I quit. It was the right decision. I'm much happier—and safer—where I am now.

Connie's decision to flee was a good one. This is what David did, and it's the best way to deal with alligators. In a book entitled *Being a Christian Friend,* Kristen Ingram inspired me with the idea of recognizing some people as being alligators. Mrs. Ingram says, "It would be foolish to go wading barefoot in the Everglades where alligators are lurking."[4]

A more accurate scriptural term than alligator is the word "fool." I'll never forget the first time I heard good teaching on the concept of a "fool" in Scripture. I was sharing the platform with Jan Silvious and she was speaking on her book, *Fool-Proofing Your Life.* (She has since told me, "I think I was born to write that book.") It has helped *so* many people who work for a fool, gave birth to a fool, or married a fool.

Before Jan's book, I was always quick to advise young women struggling in their marriages to stay, submit, and pray the marriage survives. Now I am more cautious. I realize now I have at times sent a fawn back home into the jaws of an alligator. I now draw her out with questions. If her husband exhibits the following characteristics of a fool—if he is abusive, addicted, or faithless—the kind thing for *both* of them, and the only real hope for their marriage, is to say strongly: "Separate. Set boundaries. Insist he get help and show change before you go back. You and your children are not safe. Flee."

A study of the book of Proverbs paints a vivid picture of a "fool," and we need to be aware of these characteristics. Just as you would stay away from a friend with a loaded gun and a short fuse, so should you stay away from a fool. The fool, according to Proverbs:

- **Is always right:** The way of a fool is right in his own eyes, but a wise man is he who listens to counsel (Prov. 12:15 NASB).
- **Is deceitful:** The folly of fools is deceit (Prov. 14:8 NKJV). Pours out lies (15:2).
- **Is angry and causes strife:** A fool shows his annoyance at once (Prov. 12:16); A fool's lips bring him strife (18:6); Stone is heavy and sand a burden, but provocation by a fool is heavier than both (27:3).

There is more, but if you see the above, beware. He won't repent, because he is always right. He may claim to be a believer, as Saul did, but in his heart, he says, "There is no God." We must be careful about labeling others as fools, for Jesus warns us not to call a brother a fool without cause, for that is a serious allegation. Yet if all the characteristics are there, don't go wading in the swamp. If you are already in the swamp, forgive him from your heart and flee until you see genuine change.

We should stay away from fools/alligators, but we must be sure we are dealing with an alligator, and not a rose.

Roses or Alligators?

I treated a rose like an alligator once. I fled when I should have confronted. April was sending her toddlers over to our house every day, *all* day. After six months of this, I began to plead with Steve to move to another part of the city. He finally agreed. It was a very expensive and unnecessary solution, because April wasn't an alligator. April was not trying to destroy anyone. It was just that toddlers drove her crazy and she knew I loved kids. I'd told her so!

What I never had the courage to tell her was that I also needed to have some time with my children by themselves, and so I would love having her children sometimes. I think she would have agreed to work out a schedule. Instead of being clear, I dropped hints—which she didn't catch. My failure to confront led to flight, a dropped friendship, and large moving bills. I handled it poorly. (And my sister Sally wisely said,

"Don't you realize what you've done? Your failure to confront encouraged April in her sin.")

Alligators, not roses, call for flight. Flight doesn't mean a lack of forgiveness, however. I asked Peg, who had been married to a man who left her for another woman, how she was able to keep bitterness from taking hold. The man shows no remorse, and in fact blames Peg for their failed marriage. Peg said, "I forgive him for me. I have seen how bitterness destroys people, and I'm not going to let that happen. So I forgive him for me."

Are You an Alligator?

If you recognize that you have a pattern of destruction toward others, get help from Christian professionals. In their series of radio broadcasts on abuse, Karen and David Mains stressed that you cannot break free without help. Behavior patterns can be like quicksand: The more you struggle, the deeper you go. You need someone to extend a hand. I would recommend beginning with a pastor from a Christ-centered, Bible-preaching church. How do you find a church like that? Some good questions to ask are: Are the adult Sunday school classes studying the Bible? Do most people bring and use their Bibles in church?

Although there are a myriad of reasons people become alligators, ranging from genetic temperament to childhood abuse to depression, there is one sin that has proved to be especially fertile soil for growing alligators.

Jealousy

Marie, Ann, and Leslie had become close while touring one summer with the Continentals, a Christian singing group. Marie was the most gifted, musically, of the three women: She had a lilting soprano voice with a breathtaking range. Congregations were enthralled with her solos. Ann and Leslie also were given solos, but not so frequently.

Ann accepted Marie's brighter light. Leslie tried, but as the adulation for Marie grew, Leslie found herself increasingly uncomfortable in Marie's company. She began to sit far from Marie and Ann on the bus, to ask to be placed with someone other than Marie for overnight arrangements, and grew generally uncommunicative with her formerly close friend. Marie was hurt and approached Leslie, asking her to explain why she was avoiding her. Marie told me:

My question opened a floodgate of feelings. For hours Leslie
poured out the bitterness she felt toward me. I think the time
might have been well spent had she repented of her problem. She
admitted she didn't want to have these feelings of jealousy, but
all she did was confess them; she didn't repent. I think her "confession" was designed to hurt me back—and it did. I became very
uncomfortable singing solos. I thought, "How many other people
from this group are feeling hurt, anger, and jealousy while I am
singing?" When I would be chosen for a solo, I felt regret, because
I knew there was nothing Leslie wanted more. Then, while I was
singing, despite my effort to concentrate on the Lord, I would
find myself thinking of Leslie and those like her. I became stiff
and joyless.

Novelists often portray women as being more jealous and more
backbiting than men. Perhaps we are. Perhaps our low self-esteem
makes us more vulnerable, for example, to the sin of rejoicing over
another's misfortune. How unlovely! I suspect that both men and
women struggle with feelings of jealousy, but that women are more apt
to express them.

The expression of emotion is a right-brain function. This is a
strength with emotions such as affection and compassion, but devastating with jealousy. Solomon says: "Anger is cruel and fury overwhelming,
but who can stand before jealousy?" (Prov. 27:4).

If you've ever been the victim of envy, you've tasted its cruelty.
According to Dr. Madonna Kolbenschlag, envy says, "I could forgive you
anything, except what you are; except that I am not what you are."[5]

Envy diminishes both parties: It hurts the victim and gives a hard
and bitter spirit to the perpetrator. "Envy rots the bones" (Prov. 14:30).
It destroyed Saul, and it will destroy you and me if we don't root it out
as soon as we recognize it.

It is interesting to see how differently Saul and Jonathan reacted to
David's popularity, because he was a threat to both of them. Saul was the
reigning king, and Jonathan was next in line. Yet Saul kept a jealous eye
on David and tried to destroy him, whereas Jonathan did all he could to
exalt David. What made the difference?

Saul had his eye on pleasing people, so he couldn't bear it when the
women of Israel came out to meet him with tambourines and lutes,
dancing and singing: "Saul has slain his thousands, and David his tens

of thousands" (1 Sam. 18:7). Jonathan, however, had his eye on pleasing God. He felt God's pleasure with him when he exalted David.

In a lesson on overcoming rivalry, Karen Mains said, "I think that when we feel the intimate pleasure of God, it doesn't matter how He chooses to work with our brothers and sisters."[6] I believe this is the key.

God is pleased when we can overcome our knee-jerk reaction of envy and rejoice with a successful friend. In an article entitled, "When True-Blue Turns Green," Mary Alice Kellogg tells the following story:

> Helen sounded upset: "Could we meet for lunch?" For years, we had been through all the crises that crop up when you've been friends for a long time. I was prepared to lend as much emotional support as I could and went to the restaurant expecting that something bad had happened. As it turned out, Helen did need support; she had just been named president of a hot new public relations firm, with double her previous salary and glamour to spare. A dream job. So why was she upset?
>
> "There are so few people who can hear this kind of news and truly feel glad for me," she sighed. "You're about the only friend I can genuinely share the happy news with." We toasted her success, and I reassured her that I was still her friend, even in the best of times.[7]

Gayle told me of how she and her best friend each had two sons and shared a longing to have a little girl:

> She got pregnant first, and had a third son. Then I got pregnant. When my daughter was born I was almost afraid to tell her. But when I called her, she was so excited. She brought over sacks of clothes that she had been saving for her little girl and her attitude was pure joy. I'll never forget her reaction.

I don't want to be an alligator. I want to be a rose. In fact, I long to be like Jesus, the Rose of Sharon who had absolutely no thorns. In order for that to happen, I need to be responsive to God's still, small voice.

Mary and Elizabeth were both incredibly sensitive to God, and He blessed them with a beautiful friendship. Their story has some deep truths to teach us.

CHAPTER ELEVEN

GOD KNOWS OUR NEEDS
BETTER THAN WE DO

When [Elisabeth] heard Mary's greeting, the unborn child stirred inside
her and she herself was filled with the Holy Spirit, and cried out,
"Blessed are you among women, and blessed is your child! What
an honour it is to have the mother of my Lord come to see me!
As soon as your greeting reached my ears, the child within
me jumped for joy! Oh, how happy is the woman who believes
in God, for his promises to her come true."

—LUKE 1:41–45, PH

*L*uci Shaw believes we have abandoned Mary in an "evangelical limbo."[1] Convinced that many Catholics erroneously worship Mary, many Protestants fall into the opposite error: They ignore her, except at Christmas when she is dusted off and placed in their nativity scenes. I am eager to bring Mary out of the shadows. She has so much to teach us.

Mary Said Yes to God

Jesus tells us, "For out of the overflow of the heart the mouth speaks" (Matt. 12:34). Perhaps the truest test of our character comes when our container is jostled unexpectedly. What spills out?

The angelic visit came upon Mary unawares. The announcement was one of good news and bad news: the highest honor possible for a woman intertwined with the risk of rejection by her family and fiancé.

Death by stoning was the fate for a woman caught in adultery. Mary was no adulteress, but would people believe her story?

What is this teenager's immediate reaction? One question—"How?" Hers is not a doubting, "How can I be sure of this?" as Zechariah asked when Gabriel told him Elizabeth was to be with child (Luke 1:18), but simple curiosity. "I am a virgin, so how are You going to do this, Lord?" (Who wouldn't be interested?) And then, when told, she doesn't ask for time to think about it, time to consider, she simply says, "May it be to me as you have said" (Luke 1:38). Remarkable. In an article in *Christianity Today,* Luci Shaw says, "Mary said yes to God. Perhaps God chose her ... because He knew it was her habit of life to say yes to her father and her Father."[2]

In a moment of crisis, Mary, like Ruth, desired to do what pleased God. The risks were extremely high for both of them, but in an instant they decided for God. Their attitude was, "Whatever You ask me to do, I will do it." God was pleased, and one of the ways He blessed them was through the provision of godly, earthly friends.

God's Provision of Special Friends

God knows our needs for friendships better than we do ourselves. Isabel Anders writes in a lovely article in *Partnership* of how she became friends with a woman while she was alone on a three-day visit in London:

> I had been seeing a play a day, alone. I didn't realize how lonely I was, mingling with crowds and speaking only to waitresses, cab drivers, clerks, and ticket agents. I certainly wasn't looking for a friend on my last afternoon before returning home.[3]

Before the play, Isabel had lunch in the theater tea shop. The shop was crowded, so the host asked Isabel if she would mind sharing her table with Sibyl, whom Isabel described as a sweet-faced Englishwoman. They chatted and sipped tea companionably, each enjoying the other's company. Then they parted, each to find her theater seat.

When Isabel found her seat, she was startled to see that Sibyl had the seat next to her! Sibyl seemed very glad, saying it was "fated." Isabel wrote, reflectively: "I tend to be solitary and had not realized my own need to interact with someone deeply. I began to catch on that God was giving me the gift of a friend."[4] Though Isabel was younger than Sibyl (as Mary was younger than Elizabeth), that didn't prevent her from recognizing that God might be initiating the friendship.

The play was an intensely moving one, the subject being commitment in marriage and the perils of a lack of commitment. It was a meaningful theme to each woman: Isabel was then dating the man who would be her future husband, and Sibyl was married to a "man who had been [and had put her] through much grief."[5] Touched by the play, each woman glanced at the other occasionally. Sibyl was close to tears.

After the play, Isabel and Sibyl waited in the lobby for a violent storm to subdue. The play and their sensitivity to God's hand helped them to share their lives vulnerably with each other. They discovered many threads binding them together, including the fact that they were sisters in Christ. Isabel was encouraged by the beauty of Sibyl's faith in adversity. Her thoughts may have been similar to those that Mary had about Elizabeth and the circumstances that drew them together:

> The beauty of Sibyl's faith illuminated her. The triumph of grace over adversity and God's care for her as an individual shone through, as sweetly as I've ever seen in a human face. I felt renewed strength for the life that was ahead of me—whatever it might be.
>
> How calmly we walk into the miracles of our lives—and to me, friendship is one of those miracles! How, out of all the people of the streets of London, should Sibyl and I encounter each other? God knew my needs and Sibyl's better than we had known ourselves.[6]

God knew the needs of Mary and Elizabeth better than they did themselves. Our gracious Lord made certain that Mary knew: "Even Elizabeth your relative is going to have a child in her old age, and she who was said to be barren is in her sixth month. For nothing is impossible with God" (Luke 1:36–37). And what is Mary's reaction? She recognizes God's provision of a friend in her time of need, so she hurries to see Elizabeth, and then spends three months with her providential mentor. Despite great obstacles, Mary is determined to follow through on God's leading and go to see Elizabeth.

Elizabeth was not nearby. We're told she lived in the "hill country of Judea" (Luke 1:39), which most scholars believe was probably the hills surrounding Jerusalem. This was almost one hundred miles from Nazareth. How did Mary get there? Perhaps she walked, perhaps she took a donkey. It seems she went alone. This was a long trip for Mary, and she was pregnant. Was she tired as one so often is early in pregnancy? Did she have morning sickness? (I slept fourteen hours a day during the first three months and would swoon at the sight of a hair in the sink!) But despite the distance and her pregnancy, Mary seems to have been compelled to take the trip.

Did she talk to Joseph first? I imagine so, as it's unlikely she would leave him for three months without a word. But the angel had not yet appeared to him, confirming her story that this child had been, indeed, conceived by the Holy Spirit. I suspect their parting conversation was an unsettling one, one that would further spur Mary on her arduous journey, for she knew Elizabeth would understand.

Elizabeth

God knew Elizabeth's needs as well. She had been barren all her life, and she was "well along in years" (Luke 1:7). God knew how important it was to her for this pregnancy to go well and how comforting it would be to her to see that He had done the impossible with Mary as well.

It was a disgrace to be barren in those days. Dorothy Pape, author and missionary with China Inland Mission (now Overseas Missionary Fellowship), gives us some insight on the disgrace of barrenness:

> Until very recently, in most parts of the world, a woman has been seen mainly as a baby-producing machine, as someone to perpetuate the family line of the father.... Even Martin Luther, great Christian that he was, stated, "If a woman becomes weary, or at last dies from child-bearing, that matters not; she is there to do it." For a woman not to become pregnant has usually been taken as a sign that she is displeasing to the gods and has been regarded as just grounds for divorce or the taking of a concubine.[7]

I have friends who have struggled with infertility. Often the unfulfilled longing to have a child of their own consumes them. One woman said:

> I'm always, always, dwelling on it. Every month I hope my period won't come, and then I must bear the crushing disappointment when it does. For that week and the week following I think, *We will never, never have a baby of our own.* And then, from deep inside

of me, hope springs up again, and climbs, as I think, *Maybe this month it will really happen!*

I sympathize with their pain, for my children are the delight of my life. But people today don't look upon infertile women as being without value, as they did in Elizabeth's day. Barren women then had to bear not only the sadness of not having a child of their own, but also the cultural condemnation that they had missed their lives' calling, perhaps because of disobedience!

This, of course, was not God's point of view, but man's. We know that God was pleased with Elizabeth, for we are told that she was upright in His sight (Luke 1:6). I love it that the English has two "B" words together: "blameless and barren." How much clearer could it be? Still, it was difficult for Elizabeth to bear the townspeople's clucking tongues. That's why she says, "The Lord has done this for me.... He has ... taken away my disgrace among the people" (Luke 1:25).

Not only did Elizabeth need to see the power of God as evidenced in Mary, she needed someone to talk to! Elizabeth's husband, Zechariah, had been struck dumb in the temple as discipline for not believing Gabriel's announcement. Therefore, Elizabeth was deprived of intimate conversations with her husband in anticipating the birth of their child, of a sounding board for the questions that must have come to mind, and of a prayer partner.

We are also told that Elizabeth went into seclusion for the first five months of her pregnancy. Seclusion! I like a day to myself—but five months without friends or family? Certainly during this five-month retreat Elizabeth must have drawn near to God, and perhaps that was why God led her to impose this discipline upon herself. Perhaps He wanted to mature her, to teach her to depend on Him alone, to refine her through the fire of solitary confinement. Our Father knows how easily we women fall into dependent relationships. He wanted Elizabeth to trust in Him alone. After all, He had chosen her for two crucial roles: to be a mother to John the Baptist and to be a mentor to the mother of Jesus Christ, our Lord.

Considering all this solitude, how glad Elizabeth must have been to have a visit from Mary! Mary—who could speak, who could identify closely with Elizabeth's circumstances, and who had believed God immediately! The Scripture makes it clear that Elizabeth was overjoyed to see her relative. God knew that Elizabeth and Mary would need each other, and in His mercy, in His unfailing love, He gave them to each other. And each seemed to recognize that He was giving her the gift of friendship.

Their friendship seemed part of a providential plan. Consider all the links that bound them together. Mary and Elizabeth were

- women living devoutly religious lives
- relatives, descended from King David
- experiencing miraculous pregnancies
- told their sons' names through Gabriel
- to be mothers of sons who would be great, linked in history, and destined to die horrible deaths
- each dealing with the unbelief of her husband or future husband

When we consider these links, we understand why the greeting scene between Mary and Elizabeth is perhaps the most meaningful greeting scene in all of Scripture.

The Greeting Scene

Walter Wangerin wrote: "Faith is work. It is a struggle. You must struggle with all your heart.... And on the way, God will ambush you."[8] I identify with Wangerin's play on words, for there have been times when I have been so surprised by God's response to my mustard seed of faith! Certainly it was a hard act of faith for Mary to travel one hundred miles alone to see Elizabeth, and she obviously expected some encouragement, but, oh my, what an overwhelming scene!

Can you imagine Elizabeth's emotion when she saw Mary in the doorway? No letter or phone call had warned her—this was truly a joyous surprise! And at the sound of Mary's greeting the Holy Spirit caused two additional surprises. First, John the Baptist literally leapt in his mother's womb in recognition of his Messiah in Mary's womb. This was no small stirring! Second, Elizabeth was filled with the Holy Spirit and began to prophesy. God, through Elizabeth, gave Mary the blessing she so desperately needed.

In their inspiring book *The Blessing,* Gary Smalley and John Trent tell of the great problems that befall children who grow up with parents who withhold what the Bible calls "the blessing."[9] The authors outline ways we can encourage our children, spouses, and friends with blessings. In a true blessing, a high value is attached to the person along with picturing a bright future. See how Elizabeth does this:

- "Blessed are you among women" (Luke 1:42). What higher value could be placed upon Mary? And if the friends around Mary were murmuring about her morality, how these words must have warmed her spirit! How often we withhold the encouraging word when it would mean *so much* to someone to speak it.

- "And blessed is the child you will bear!" (Luke 1:42). It must have been *so* encouraging to Mary to realize Elizabeth already knew about the baby and who He was. God was definitely in this. If Mary's thoughts needed to be lifted beyond her temporary distress to the treasure she was carrying, Elizabeth does it here.

- "But why am I so favored, that the mother of my Lord should come to me?" (Luke 1:43). Though Elizabeth, because of her age, would normally be given more reverence than Mary, here she is bowing her knee to Mary. ("Bow the knee" is what the Hebrew word for blessing means.) Too often it is pride that keeps us from speaking the encouraging word.

- "Blessed is she who has believed that what the Lord has said to her will be accomplished!" (Luke 1:45). Elizabeth knows through the Holy Spirit that Mary, unlike Joseph and unlike Zechariah, immediately believed God! And this *blessed* is a Greek word meaning satisfied, fulfilled, full of God. Elizabeth is saying, "Good for you, Mary, you believed! And because of that, your future is going to hold joy and fulfillment." What faith do you see in your friends that you could affirm?

This was a blessing that Mary would forever treasure in her heart. In response, Mary sings her hauntingly lovely "Magnificat." Some commentators cannot believe she composed this song. It is loaded with Old Testament references, and they say that it is too brilliant for a woman, so Luke must have written it! Others believe Elizabeth sang it.

But the Scripture clearly states that Mary was the singer! The joy, the ecstasy, and the praise for her Savior that flow from her lips give us one of the clearest portraits of just how godly Mary was.

Mary says, "His mercy extends to those who fear him, from generation to generation" (Luke 1:50). The Greek word translated "mercy" is as close as you can get in the Greek to the Hebrew word *hesed* (unfailing love). And haven't we seen the truth of Mary's words? God's unfailing love has flowed from Naomi to her daughter-in-law, Ruth; from Ruth to her descendant, David; and from David to his descendant, Mary! They feared God, and He blessed them mightily, from generation to generation!

Never Is Heard a Discouraging Word

I can imagine a very different scenario had Mary and Elizabeth not been the godly women they were. When I was first married, I was surprised to find that some women commonly disparaged their husbands to other women. (I wasn't a Christian at that time, and neither were my friends.) Perhaps that was due, in part, to the fact that many of my friends were wives of medical students and were weary of their husbands' schedules. Together they would augment their husbands' weaknesses in their minds, chipping away at the foundations of their marriages. No wonder Scripture admonishes wives to respect their husbands!

Had Mary and Elizabeth not been women who loved and feared God, they might have commiserated about the lack of spirituality of men and about the lack of faith Joseph and Zechariah had demonstrated.

When we were studying Mary and Elizabeth during a Bible study, one woman had the following insight into her own behavior:

> I'm not likely to criticize a friend's husband, but I am not so gracious when it comes to my brother-in-law, Jeff. Though Jeff is really quite a nice chap, I'm extremely protective of my little sister and I want the very best for her and my nephews. The Lord has been showing me through this study that my criticism has actually hurt my sister's marriage more than any of Jeff's flaws, because I've encouraged her to think less of her husband.

Elizabeth undoubtedly had protective feelings for her young cousin, but she doesn't utter a discouraging word about Joseph. As friends (and as mothers-in-law) we have a choice: We can either encourage women to think well of their husbands, or we can help them to be like the foolish woman of the proverb, who tears down her house with her own hands (Prov. 14:1).

Of course it is a far different situation if a woman is married to an abusive or unfaithful man. Then we need to listen with hearing ears and counsel separation. But usually, a woman is simply venting the normal feelings that occur in marriage. Men and women are different, and we are all sinners, so conflict is inevitable.

Mary Treasured Up All These Things

Both Elizabeth and Mary had a great deal of pain coming in their futures. If Elizabeth was still alive when John the Baptist was an adult, she had to relinquish him to the wilderness and then bear the pain of his murder, for he was beheaded for speaking out against the adulterous relationship Herod had with his brother's wife.

Mary, too, would face more heartache than most of us will ever know. Her name is derived from a Hebrew word meaning "bitterness." Luci Shaw writes:

> From the hour of Announcement on, dark pain lay ahead—friends' incredulity, lack of understanding, accusations of promiscuity, and her son's illegitimacy, to begin with.[10]

After her visit with Elizabeth, Mary made the long trip home to Nazareth, only to turn around several months later to trek back to Bethlehem in Judea. Luci continues:

> She and Joseph were poor, and even if they had a donkey to ride, a blanket on the back of an ass is no easy seat for a woman nine-months pregnant, her body cold and stiff from sitting on the plodding animal for hours at a time.
>
> Bethlehem, in turn, seemed so harsh and unwelcoming in the winter night. Perhaps her first uneasy cramping of labor had begun, and the panic of helplessness as the busy innkeeper turned them away.[11]

Mixed with these moments of fear and pain were moments of absolute exaltation—her time with Elizabeth, the star above the manger, the visit of the Magi! Luci says that Mary needed "the exhilaration of these days to balance the pain of the next thirty-three years and beyond."[12] Wisely, Mary "treasured up all these things and pondered

them in her heart" (Luke 2:19). Life is mixed with moments of pain
and joy. If we have been keeping a treasure chest (perhaps in the form
of a journal of answers to prayer), we can dig it out during bleak times.
Peg said:

> When my husband was planning to leave me, and then when he
> did, the Lord seemed so very near to me, showing me His unfail-
> ing love in amazing ways day after day. Through the love of
> friends, through the ways He was obviously trying to get my hus-
> band's attention, and through His presence, so unmistakably real,
> so strong.
>
> But now, sometimes, the road seems so lonely, and I ques-
> tion: *Was God really with me? Or was I imagining it?* I need to go
> back to my treasure chest and look over those moments of
> epiphany again.

I believe that during those three months that Mary spent with
Elizabeth, each gave the other moments for their treasure chests. By
sharing their joy, they doubled it. God knew that each would need
these moments to remember and treasure, for He could see the dark
road ahead. God knows our needs better than we do ourselves.

God Knows How Much We Can Carry

My friend Pat is a missionary with International Students Incorporated
and a wonderfully warm and strong Christian woman. One day she
said, with a twinkle in her eye, "Dee, I'm not going to ask God to give
me friends anymore."

"But, why?" I inquired.

"Because I've done that three times, and three times the Lord has
given me a friend who needed me a whole lot more than I needed her!"

I laughed, because I realized (as did Pat) that God knew exactly what
He was doing. He knew Pat had the strength and wisdom to help hurting women. God may lead us to disheartened friends, for He knows
what we can handle and what we can't. (And then we have the choice
to follow through in obedience or to flee.) God knows our strengths and
our needs better than we do.

God knows if you or I have the ability to be a friend to a younger
woman—as Elizabeth was to Mary—and to give her light for the dark
road ahead. And though the desire of our heart may be to have a friend

who is a peer, it may be the desire of God's heart for us to be a mentor to a younger friend, and He may bring her across our path. Isn't it at least interesting that both of the models of feminine friendship in Scripture are between women of different generations? And though we seem to assume that the benefit would be largely on the younger woman's part, that isn't necessarily so. Elizabeth was greatly blessed by Mary, as was Naomi by Ruth.

Let's consider the idea of finding or being a mentor, for it is one of the basic concepts in Scripture concerning the friendships of women, and it is a concept that, if applied, could dramatically change your life.

CHAPTER TWELVE

THE MENTOR RELATIONSHIP

On Christmas Eve, a deep San Francisco-style fog kept our car crawling blindly along the road. Suddenly another car pulled onto the road right ahead of us. Because we were now following a set of beautiful twin taillights, we could safely increase our speed from fifteen to twenty-five miles an hour. A mentor is someone further on down the road from you who is going where you want to go and who is willing to give you some light to help you get there.[1]

*M*y sister Bonnie was nineteen; I was fifteen. We were walking back to our family's cottage from the village of Ephraim, Wisconsin, a picturesque resort town of white buildings nestled on a hill overlooking the gleaming waters of Green Bay. A black '55 Thunderbird flashed by, and then suddenly my sister became unhinged: "That was Jim Rock's car! I'm sure it was! He's driven all the way up here to see me, and he's trying to find our cottage—I know it, I know it!" We dashed madly through the wooded road so that Bonnie could comb her hair and put on fresh lipstick. Bonnie was right. Jim Rock, whom she'd met only once, was coming for an extended visit.

As the days passed, Bonnie worried that our parents might think Jim's visit was too long. Out of concern that Jim might outwear his welcome, Bonnie told her suitor what Benjamin Franklin had said: "Fish and visitors smell in three days." Jim decided to leave promptly! But, he was not deterred from his intentions, for he eventually married my sister—and, I should add, has good-naturedly listened to the telling of this tale for forty years!

With this memory from my childhood, my initial reaction to the discovery that Mary spent three months with Elizabeth was, "Three months! Perhaps someone should have given Mary a nudge about her manners!"

I asked Win Couchman, who is a retreat speaker on the subject of cross-generational relationships, what she thought about Mary's three-month visit. She told me that having a Filipino daughter-in-law has helped her to understand the story of Mary's visit to Elizabeth. Win said,

> Lengthy visits and visits away from fiancé or husband seem so natural to her. And especially natural would be the visit between two pregnant relatives. There is an extremely open sharing between women in a family that I have been learning, to my delight, from this precious provincial woman. Her view of time is so different. Three months? A short visit.

Now, as I am growing in my appreciation of the value of mentors, I realize that God planned this lengthy visit to help Mary prepare for the dark and unique obstacles on the road ahead.

Elizabeth, Mary's Mentor

Elizabeth means "worshipper of God." We are told she led a blameless (blameless!) life. Jill Briscoe noted that Elizabeth is the kind of woman who, as you stand before her, convicts you by her life and challenges you by her faith.[2]

Mary would soon be a wife, so she watched with interest just how a godly couple related to each other in marriage. She and Joseph would not have the balm of a sexual relationship to soothe them during their first months of marital adjustment. (There was an interesting debate in England in 1985 concerning giving contraceptives to teenagers. The negative side was headed by an eloquent English mother. She said that encouraging teens in premarital sex uses up their "balm." She explained that during the difficult first year of marriage, when a couple is adjusting to each other, they need that balm of tremendous sexual excitement to soothe the hurts they unintentionally inflict on each other.)

Mary and Joseph had not used up their balm, but they would not be using it, as there were to be no sexual relations until after Jesus was born. Mary and Joseph were going to need, instead, the balms of kindness, tenderness, and trust in God. And I believe God built up this balm in Mary by providing her with a mentor, by having her spend three months with a devout older woman who showed respect and love for her husband.

When speaking in California, I referred to "the balm" of tremendous sexual excitement, which God has given to newlyweds. Afterward, a glowing little lady in her nineties came up and fairly shouted to me: "I LIKED YOUR POINT ABOUT THE BOMB!"

"The bomb?" I was confused.

"YES!" she repeated emphatically. "I REMEMBER! IT WAS A BOMB!"

Mary knew the Scriptures, as evidenced by her Magnificat. Elizabeth had just come out of five months of seclusion with the Lord. Both must have been eager to feast on the other's knowledge of prophecy. Can you imagine what it would be like to be pregnant with a child whose destiny was predicted in Scripture? And how caring of God to provide this sharpening time for Mary and Elizabeth to prepare for a future filled with joy and sorrow?

Elizabeth probably gave Mary help in practical matters as well. How delightful it must have been to be with a friend who was pregnant, as you were, and to know you were both carrying sons! I can picture them dying material blue together, sewing a layette, and talking all the time about how to rear boys!

And finally, before Mary headed back to Nazareth, I think she helped in the delivery of John the Baptist. She did not know, at this time, that she would be giving birth in a stable; but God knew, and I'm convinced He provided her with seeing a baby born, the umbilical cord tied and cut, and the baby washed and wrapped in swaddling clothes. God knew Mary's needs better than she did.

The Value of Mentors

Karen Mains reminisced about a seventy-year-old nun who cleaned her house when Karen was a young mother. The only payment Theresa would accept was that of bus fare. Every time the clock hit the quarter hour, Theresa would pray. Threads of prayer were intricately woven into the fabric of her life. Karen says, "I think of her now with tears. I am certain that she built something into my life that I'm beginning to reap and see the benefit of now."[3]

Steve and I came to Christ while he was going through medical school, so we experienced great spiritual riches simultaneously with material poverty! During that time I became pregnant, and an older woman from our church (she was probably in her thirties—but she was older to me) stopped by to visit. Having met Bev only briefly, I was curious about the reason for her visit. Bev told me she wanted to make maternity clothes for me. I had trouble comprehending that she didn't want money or anything else in return but simply wanted to serve me in Christian love. I had never experienced this kind of friendship! Bev provided me with a vital model that the Christian life was much more than Christ meeting our needs; but it was a commitment to serve Him daily.

An older woman who is truly living the Christian life can be a tremendous model to a younger woman. If they spend time together, the younger woman can pick up, as if by osmosis, how she should live. Win Couchman tells about observing Mary Lou, who has been a mentor to Win:

> At Mary Lou's eightieth birthday party, I noticed that she was in very dignified black and white tweed. I decided to tease her a little about being so dignified now that she's eighty. Mary Lou stuck a finger under my nose and said, "You're not very observant today, Win! Take a look at the purse and the shoes!" I looked, and behold, red patent leather! ... Then she took me in the back room and, dimpling, said, "Now, Win, there has to be a balance. Yes, I must be dignified. I am eighty. But I'm myself too!" And she flipped up just enough of the corner of her skirt to let me see the over-the-knee red underwear.[4]

Win says Mary Lou has been a beacon to her, that she has modeled a tenderness toward God, and yet also fun in life—so many things that Win wants to be or do when she is further on down the road of life.

Mentors in the Career World

In *Mentors and Protégés,* Linda Phillips-Jones gives many examples of experienced career women who were eager to encourage less-experienced women. She tells of Katherine S. White, the late fiction editor of *The New Yorker,* who was known for the unshakable faith she had in her writers and who nurtured them on to better writing. "When White died, the magazine was deluged with letters that praised her and described the profound effect that her deep sense of caring had on people's lives."[5]

Grace, a young dynamic black lawyer, said of her mentor, "Her rules of personal behavior keep her ethically way above those around her. It really helps me to have her around as a kind of mirror."[6]

Successful godly women in the career world are rare, but nothing is impossible for God, so pray persistently for a mentor. He knows your needs better than you do.

Mothers-in-Law and Daughters-in-Law

In your family, a mother, an older sister, an aunt, or even a mother-in-law can serve as a mentor. I'm no longer amused by mother-in-law jokes—and I'm distressed, as the mother of two sons, that they are usually targeted at the mother of the son. I've pondered: *What are some of the root problems that create ugly mother-in-law situations?*

Dr. James Dobson says that one of the reasons a woman feels more anxiety about letting a son go rather than a daughter is because the son is less apt to keep close contact. There's some sad truth in the saying, "A son is a son 'til he takes a wife, but a daughter's a daughter the rest of her life."[7] Because women have a gift for nurturing relationships, they're less likely to emotionally abandon their parents: They're more faithful in writing, calling, visiting, and expressing affection.

A mother is also going to feel more replaced by a daughter-in-law than she would by a son-in-law. It seems to me that the key is following Naomi's model. I have determined in my heart to remember how much Ruth and Orpah loved Naomi. If Naomi had feelings of jealousy when her sons married, she rooted them out and loved Ruth and Orpah as if they were her very own. What a beautiful, inspiring relationship! As a future mother-in-law, I gain hope from Naomi.

I've also been encouraged by the relationship my sister Bonnie had with her mother-in-law. I didn't realize how much Lillian meant to her until after Lillian's death. Bonnie is a blithe spirit, energetic and cheerfully eager about each day, seldom heavy-hearted. The exception, which surprised us all, was the year following her mother-in-law's death. My sister was devastated. Seven years later, as Bonnie and I sat on the beach together, I asked her to tell me why she loved Lillian so much. Her words tumbled out, and even then, after so much time, tears welled up in my normally dry-eyed sister:

> Everybody loved Lillian! Just being near her was a comfort and a lift. Her humor, her joy in life, her attentiveness to your thoughts and feelings, her quiet faith. Lillian spent three months living with us one time. My friends raised their eyebrows and said, "Three months? Three months with your mother-in-law in the same house?" But it wasn't a difficult time. It is a joyous, precious memory in our lives. It helped that she was sensitive to both my need for privacy and my need for help. She would take long walks. She would completely stay out of the kitchen during preparation time. She said two cooks was one too many—so instead she would talk to the kids. I liked that. Then, afterward, she would insist on cleaning up by herself. But I think I was drawn to her because of the way she loved me. I didn't feel like a daughter-in-law but like a beloved daughter. Her actions, her eyes, and her smile told me— but if I didn't know, she wasn't hesitant to express it. If she sensed I was troubled she would say, "I hope you know how very much I love you." ... I miss her so much.

It is also vital that daughters-in-law give their mothers-in-law a chance. I remember thinking as a newlywed that my mother-in-law should have it all together because she was so old. Now that I *am* a mother-in-law, I am *so much more sympathetic*. I was forty-four when John married Julie, and I was still very good at putting my foot in my mouth.

Fortunately, John was quick to tell me, "You hurt Julie when you ..." But even though there were times I hurt her, times when I didn't make her feel valued, Julie responded with grace. Grace is not natural—when my mother-in-law hurt me, I wanted to withdraw. When *I* hurt Julie, instead of withdrawing, she gave me love. Because Julie gave me grace, today we are very close and I truly see her, not as a daughter-in-law, but as a daughter.

As daughters-in-law, we need to become as vulnerable as Ruth. She told her mother-in-law everything! Jill Briscoe said that the biggest problem she sees in the relationships between mothers-in-law and daughters-in-law is lack of communication. We go so far, but hold our mothers-in-law at arm's length, unwilling to be like Ruth and go all the way to Bethlehem.[8] Ruth also gave Naomi amazing grace. When Naomi kept sending her home, when Naomi said she was "empty" despite Ruth's companionship and commitment, Ruth gave Naomi grace. What a model she is to us as daughters-in-law.

Mentoring Is Informal

In discipling, you meet with someone regularly to learn how to study the Bible, pray, and serve—but while mentoring may include some of this, it tends to be much less formal. It's not to be a dependent relationship, but simply a friendship as you spend time with a woman who is further down the road, at least in some areas of her Christian life.

Win Couchman says, "Mentoring works very nicely over a cup of coffee."[9] I frequently had tea with Miriam, my ninety-year-old neighbor in Seattle. What a woman of God she was: given to diligent prayer, hospitality, and nurturing children into the kingdom. She showed me how to seize the tremendous opportunity of caring for others' children. Our daughter Sally, who was then just a toddler, loved Miriam. (Sally received letters from Miriam until Miriam went to be with Jesus.) Whenever Sally would come back from a visit with Miriam, she'd have a verse of Scripture memorized and a lemon drop. (I think there was a connection.)

I was also impressed with how thankful, how content, Miriam was with her small home. I identified with the feelings expressed from a young woman in a letter to Win Couchman:

> Your love of homemaking freed me to indulge my lifelong desire to be a homemaker. You demonstrated creativity in recipes, menus, and decoration of your modest home. This encouraged me not to covet bigger and better home and furnishings, but to express my personality and creative ideas in my home.[10]

My friend Maureen Rank, author of *Free to Grieve,* sat with me at a writer's conference where we heard Karen Mains comment that she divides herself up and has several mentors. Maureen whispered, "That seems much healthier than having just one mentor who becomes God to you." I agree. One woman excels in raising children, another in hospitality, another in Bible knowledge. I can have a composite mentor by asking questions and taking the initiative to spend time with each of several women.

Today we have resources through the Internet as well. I have loved the free Internet program *www.settingcaptivesfree.com*—not only is there a daily Bible study, but a mentor is assigned to you to encourage and advise through e-mail. I have done it for the food program (The Lord's Table) but there are other programs as well.

When you finish the program with success, you in turn are allowed the opportunity to mentor another. I also have a mentor when I take seminary classes online with Covenant Seminary. Simply being accountable and receiving encouragement helps me to follow through in a way I might not have if I were alone. If there is a woman you respect and you would like advice and guidance, ask her if you could e-mail her about some of your work, parenting, or dating questions.

The Younger Woman Should Take the Initiative

Win believes that it's best if the younger woman takes the initiative in asking to spend time and to observe. It may begin with a simple request such as asking for help in making an apple pie or in balancing a budget. It may begin by the younger woman asking the older woman to share some of her wisdom.

As a young mother, I asked a woman in Oregon how she had managed to raise her three teenage boys so that they loved the Lord so passionately. Her sons stood apart from their peers in the steadfastness of their walk, and I was particularly impressed because I knew their father was an atheist. She answered me carefully, and I'll never forget her words: "Dee, I can't say anything at home. I've never been able to. So I pray. Oh, do I pray! For an hour on my knees, every morning."

Younger women often run to their peers to discuss child-raising, marriage, or life. How much wiser if they would look to a woman who has done it well, and run to her. Otherwise it is the blind leading the blind—and you may both fall into a pit. It's always hard to approach someone, for you may be refused, but if you simply ask her if you can spend some time together (rather than asking her to "mentor" you), you may find she is delighted.

Mentoring Blesses Both the Mentor and the Mentee

In the spring after the winter of her husband's death, Luci Shaw was the speaker at a poet's workshop in Seattle. Margaret Smith was one of the students, and she longed to develop a more personal friendship with this woman with whom she had corresponded. But because Luci was a generation older than Margaret, and well known, Margaret was unsure how Luci would respond to an overture of friendship. But Margaret decided to risk inviting Luci to spend a few days at her Oregon home following the conference.

Margaret told me, with obvious delight, "Luci said yes!" Why did Luci agree? Partly because she liked Margaret and had hoped to know her better, but also because Luci is aware of her responsibility to young and promising poets. We need more women like Luci, who, having succeeded in their fields (whether writing poetry, climbing the corporate ladder, or raising children who love the Lord), are willing to have a mentor relationship with a younger woman. Margaret calls Luci, "Wise One." Luci said, laughing, "So I'm working on being wise."

A mentor relationship is obviously of great value to the younger woman, but it can be equally rewarding to the older woman. It is reciprocal. Ruth certainly was a blessing to Naomi, standing by her, empathizing with her sorrow. I believe that Margaret similarly blessed Luci, who, like Naomi, had just been widowed in midlife. One night during Luci's stay, Margaret, in an exercise of her gift for empathy, marked the following lines from a poem by George Herbert:

> And now in age I bud again;
> After so many deaths I live and write;
> I once more smell the dew and rain,
> And relish versing. O my only Light,
> It cannot be
> That I am [s]he
> On whom Thy tempests fall all night.

Believing the passage would minister to her grieving friend, Margaret left the book of Herbert's poetry open on Luci's bedside table. Through the medium of the poem, she was recognizing Luci's pain, acknowledging the tempest that had fallen on her, and affirming the truth of renaissance, of new life and growth after bereavement. The poem not only showed empathy, it gave wisdom and encouragement as it pointed to the truth that God, our "only Light," is the source of renewal and comfort.

Margaret found a pensive Luci walking behind the house early the next morning, looking out beyond the stretch of rhododendrons and sea oats to the spruces that lined the Skipanon River. Margaret wrote a poem about this moment in their friendship:

> I found her out
> by the garden,
> watching the river and woods—
> I called her from hard dreaming ...

Margaret went and stood beside Luci. Together they watched the flashes of indigo in the woods as stellar jays darted among the spruces. Luci said, "Those lines from Herbert—that's just it." Empathizing, Margaret wrote further:

> Someone should be able
> to hold her
> grief, take it
> like a knapsack of rocks,
> let her tiptoe
> give wings to
> fly with no gravity.

Margaret longed to hold some of Luci's pain. And she did, in part, by understanding. Such empathy erases the boundaries of age. Margaret said, "Although Luci is my mother's age, she's not like a mom. She's just a friend."

Older Women Aren't So Very Different

My cousin Diane was disillusioned with the single life in Los Angeles. Remembering the beauty of her childhood summers in Ephraim, Wisconsin, she uprooted herself and moved there. Life was much quieter in this town that boasted "Population: 319." Because there weren't any women her age, Diane was forced to develop friendships with older women. I asked her what it was like. Reflectively, she said:

> Once I got over the fact that these women were older, I stopped seeing that. They simply became my friends. I'm amazed, sometimes, how close we are. Because I am single, and have no children, I have actually found that there is a bigger division between married women who are my age than there is between married women who are a generation older. Since their children are grown, they are not so caught up in their children. We can talk about other subjects.

Wrinkles, gray hair, and a matronly figure should not obscure the reality that these women have been where you are going, and in their struggles with sin, with the joys and difficulties of sex, and with careers and relationships, they have gained some valuable wisdom. If you are aware of an older woman whom you admire for her walk with Christ, ask her if you could spend some time with her informally. Be careful not to take advantage, be careful to respect her commitments, but ask for permission to observe.

Older Women Need to Be Open

Karen Mains says, "It is time for those of us in our forties and fifties to begin being responsible for our own adult spiritual age. We need to set ourselves aside in order to become so filled with God that He will make us women of great spiritual power."[11] It's not optional on the older woman's part to be willing, for Scripture commands it. She may have to limit the number of younger women she can mentor at any one time, but she needs to be approachable. Paul mentions several things the older women should be modeling for the younger women. He stresses that the older women should be reverent in the way they live, not to be slanderers, or addicted to much wine, and they are to teach what is good. What is good? Paul spells that out clearly:

> They should be examples of the good life, so that the younger women may learn to love their husbands and their children, to be sensible and chaste, home-lovers, kindhearted and willing to adapt themselves to their husbands—a good advertisement for the Christian faith. (Titus 2:4–5 PH)

Some churches permanently divide adult Sunday school classes according to age. This makes it difficult for the older women to teach the younger. If this is your situation, become involved in a Christ-centered Bible study group that doesn't have age divisions. In these, older women often will teach younger women "to love their husbands and their children," as Titus 2 commands them to do. Phyllis held the younger women spellbound when she shared:

> When our children were young, my desire for sexual intimacy with my husband waned. It felt like a duty and I was resentful that after all day with the kids he would ask one more thing of me, and I was resentful of the Scripture that said I shouldn't deprive my

husband of sexual relations (see 1 Cor. 7:3–5). But one day, in my quiet time, I saw that Scripture in a new light. The reason we aren't to deprive each other was so that Satan wouldn't get a toehold in our lives. I began to repent—not just by agreeing physically, but in my spirit. I was amazed at how God poured out the blessings on our marriage, renewing me, and giving me more joy and energy for all I had to do. We can be to our husbands like the Shulamite maiden in the Song of Solomon was, if we just choose to be!

Though it may be best for the younger woman to initiate the mentor relationship, the older woman can demonstrate that she is open. Beryl, a woman in her sixties, sends cards and notes of encouragement to younger women. One young woman told me, "I have a stack of cards from Beryl—encouraging notes with timely Scriptures—which lifted me up at needy times in my life."

The first time I met Beryl was on the telephone. We were new in town and Steve had just begun his medical practice. Beryl called and asked if I was Dr. Brestin's wife. When I answered affirmatively, she said, "I want you to know I'm in love with your husband." Then she broke into my shocked silence with her warm, loving laugh. "I also want you to know I'm old enough to be his mother." She then went on to explain that she had fervently prayed, as she sat in the ambulance next to her mother, for a tender, compassionate, patient doctor. "Your husband was God's gracious answer to my prayer."

Beryl was teaching me to love my husband. She also showed me the door was open for friendship, and in walking through I have been tremendously encouraged by her model. Beryl has shown me God's love, joy, and patience as I've watched her delight in her twenty-eight-year-old son, who has Down's syndrome.

Women are exhorted, in Titus 2, to be mentors. The closest female friendships in Scripture are, indeed, mentoring ones (Ruth and Naomi; Mary and Elizabeth). When something is repeated in Scripture, it is because the Lord God is emphasizing its importance. Let us consider, in the closing chapter, the important lessons He has repeated in regard to friendship. If you embrace these truths with all your mind, heart, and strength—you will experience the power of friendship. You will also become a reflection of Christ.

CHAPTER THIRTEEN

REFLECTIONS OF CHRIST

Salutation (St. Luke 1:39–45)
Framed in light,
Mary sings through the doorway.
Elizabeth's six month joy jumps,
a palpable greeting, a hidden first encounter
between son and Son.
And my heart turns over when I meet Jesus
in you.[1]

—LUCI SHAW

*A*s you put God's friendship pattern into practice, a transforma-
tion will take place in you. Because each of the characteristics in
God's pattern are actually characteristics of Christ, you will become
Christ's reflection in the world, as were Ruth, David, and Mary. We've
looked at eleven threads that have wound their way through the tapestry
of the three scriptural models of friendship we've examined, and I'd like
to review each of these threads and give you an opportunity to reflect on
how you might apply them specifically in your life.

Greeting Scenes

By "greeting scenes," I mean the sensitivity to realize, on meeting someone, that God may be involved. God knows our needs better than we do
and wants us to be alert to the people we meet.

Ruth, Jonathan, and Mary were alert to the friends God placed in their path. All crossed high hurdles to establish those friendships because they believed God was leading.

In the rewriting of this book, I have had the chance to reflect on five friends who became perennial (lifelong, season-after-season friends). I realize that four of the five were friends I had asked God for, and then He crossed their paths with mine.

How sensitive are you to those you meet for the first time? Do you ask, when you meet them, whether it could be that God has a reason for bringing this person across your path?

Dependence on God More Than a Friend

Rachel said that the root problem leading to lesbianism is "worshipping" a person rather than God, a dependency on another person. Likewise, Naomi expected men to fulfill her needs, and when the men were gone, she was devastated.

As women, our tendency toward dependency on people is our Achilles' heel. We engage in "relational idolatry" with both friends and husbands, forgetting that our only real security is in God. In our desire to secure our bond, we are tempted by sins such as gossip and betrayal. When we or a soul mate moves, we feel like our foundation is crumbling.

When Steve told me were going to leave Seattle, I sobbed out my misery to my sister Sally on the telephone.

Sally said, "Dee, calm down. Do you know where your real home is?"

"Seattle!" I sobbed. "My friends are here, my church is here, my home is here."

"Your real home, Dee," my sister wisely said, "is in heaven. You are just passing through and Seattle was a temporary tent stop." As Sally lifted my eyes beyond the horizons of this earth to heaven and my real home, I realized she was speaking the truth. The temporal things will pass away, and we need to place our feet securely on the solid rock of Jesus Christ. It's important to love our friends and to be committed to them. But we need to be dependent on God, because He's the only One who will never leave us. God taught me this through His friendship pattern, knowing how desperately I would need it when I became a young widow.

It should encourage us to see how Ruth, David, and Mary depended on God and found Him absolutely faithful. I have as well. He has truly become my Provider, Protector, and Confidante.

In order to be like Christ and the models in whom we've seen Him reflected, consider this: Are you willing to share a soul mate? To divide a growing Bible study? To refuse to gossip? To trust that God will provide when your best friend moves?

An Intertwining of Intuition with Holy Spirit Power

Intuition is a right-brain function and most women are blessed with it. Obviously, there are times when we're going to be wrong, but if we check our hunches by leaning on the Holy Spirit (by being immersed in the Scriptures and sensitive to His quiet voice), we will be wise to move ahead when something seems "good to the Holy Spirit and to us" (Acts 15:28).

I believe this is what Ruth did when she read between the lines of Naomi's rejection and stood by her side. Likewise, Mary seemed to know that it was important to take the hundred-mile trip to see Elizabeth.

In order to use your gift of intuition wisely in friendship, let me ask you: Are you reading through the Bible regularly? Are you memorizing Scripture regularly? The Holy Spirit never conflicts with the Word, so this must be the starting point. We know, for example, that Scripture exhorts us to encourage one another, carry one another's burdens, and speak the truth in love. But knowing *when* and to *whom* to apply these principles involves an intertwining of intuition with Holy Spirit power.

For example, I just had my first birthday without Steve. How comforted I was by the women who intuitively knew it would be a hard day and obeyed the Holy Spirit in finding ways to bless me. Jayne sent fragrant flowers; Bonnie took me to lunch; and Kathy is helping me do an extreme makeover of a room in my cottage. This birthday, they knew, needed an extra dose of love.

Risk-Taking

Risk-taking is essential for finding friends and bonding with them. Ruth, Jonathan, and Mary took tremendous risks in initiating friendships and then in making themselves vulnerable. Christ risked dying on the cross, even though many would not respond.

One young woman wrote: "I received *The Friendships of Women* as a high-school graduation gift and read it that summer. I am so glad because I tend to be a shrinking violet. But I was determined to be friendly to the girls in my college dorm, especially those in whom I saw admirable qualities. I initiated conversations, I asked if I could join someone at their table in the cafeteria, and I affirmed women when I saw lovely character-istics in them. I made wonderful friends, and my time at college was definitely one of the sweetest times in my life."

In order to be like Christ and the models in whom we've seen Him reflected, consider: Will you risk reaching out to someone you admire? And if someone does not at first respond to you, will you try again?

Unfailing Love

Naomi prayed that God would show Ruth unfailing love (Ruth 1:8), and Jonathan said to David, "Show me unfailing kindness like that of the LORD" (1 Sam. 20:14).

We are living in a time of impermanence and easy good-byes. It takes discipline to show unfailing love when a friend is needing a great deal of help or when she moves away or when she hurts you with unkind words. But how like Christ, who shows us His faithfulness morning by morning, we become if we can show steadfast kindness in these situations!

When someone goes through a crisis, as I did when Steve died, friends are put through an automatic test. Some came forth as gold: weeping with me, attending the funeral, skipping the sermons, praying faithfully, and remembering the man I love by talking about him. Others tried and failed with awkward sermonettes or with inquiries of my well-being. (*No! Give me time!* I wanted to say.) Then there were friends who didn't write, come, or call. I *do* forgive them, for I have been forgiven so much. But a crisis automatically makes you reevaluate your closest circle of friends.

In order to be like Christ and the models in whom we have seen Him reflected, consider: Have you assessed your true connections? How will you discipline yourself to remain true to your real connections nearby? How will you respond if a close friend lets you down?

Sharing Vulnerably

After her night with Boaz, Ruth told Naomi "everything." Jonathan and David bared their souls to each other, and Elizabeth didn't tone down her ecstasy in seeing Mary.

In Gethsemane, Jesus vulnerably told Peter, James, and John that He needed their support and prayer. He said, "My soul is overwhelmed with sorrow to the point of death" (Mark 14:34).

Do you remember Ann Kiemel's observation? She found that "being vulnerable actually draws people to us, because the world is full of people … that are bleeding and hurting."[2]

Will you strip away pretenses with trusted friends? Will you be trustworthy with their confidences?

Whatever You Ask Me to Do, I'll Do It

Ruth spoke these words to Naomi when Naomi proposed her daring plan (Ruth 3:5). And Jonathan said the same thing to David when David asked him to risk his life to find out Saul's true motives (1 Sam. 20:4). And Christ has said to us, "You may ask me for anything in my name, and I will do it" (John 14:14).

This pattern intrigues me: It shows me how careful I should be in making requests of soul mates, but also how responsive I should be when a close friend asks for help. It is particularly hard for a hurting friend to ask for help, but if she even hints, we should respond with, "Whatever you ask me to do, I'll do it."

Will you respond cheerfully and eagerly, despite great personal sacrifice, when a friend asks for help?

Words of Blessing or Encouragement

Repeatedly, our scriptural friends "blessed" one another verbally. Note the pattern in the following examples: the high value that is attributed to the friend and the bright future that is pictured, often through prayer, because of God's faithfulness.

Naomi to Ruth and Orpah: "May the LORD show kindness [unfailing love] to you, as you have shown to your dead and to me" (Ruth 1:8).

Boaz to Ruth: "All my fellow townsmen know that you are a woman of noble character" (Ruth 3:11); "May you be richly rewarded by the LORD, the God of Israel, under whose wings you have come to take refuge" (Ruth 2:12).

Jonathan to David, when he "helped him find strength in God" at Horesh: "Don't be afraid.... My father Saul will not lay a hand on you. You will be king over Israel, and I will be second to you" (1 Sam. 23:17).

Elizabeth to Mary: "Blessed is she who has believed that what the Lord has said to her will be accomplished!" (Luke 1:45).

How sensitive are you to blessing the people in your life?

Intergenerational Friendship

Although David and Jonathan were peers, the friendships between Ruth and Naomi and between Mary and Elizabeth were intergenerational friendships. This should speak to us, as should God's command that the older women teach the younger. It is likewise interesting that in both cases the friends were also relatives, though mentors aren't limited to relatives.

How open are you to being approached by a younger woman in order to spend some time with her informally? And have you considered approaching a godly older woman for advice or help in ministering in the community or simply to have tea together?

Parting Scenes

God zoomed His camera in on parting scenes between Ruth and Naomi and then again with David and Jonathan. As we watch them weep and cling to each other, we understand Shakespeare's words, "Parting is such sweet sorrow."[3]

Likewise, Scripture shows us that Christ did not shrink from saying good-bye to those He loved. He began saying good-bye very early in His three-year ministry, warning them that He would be crucified. His words "Do not let your hearts be troubled" (John 14:1) remind me of Jonathan's parting words to David. Words and emotions that are expressed in parting scenes come to our remembrance again and again. Parting scenes, though painful, are not wasted sadness.

Since the original edition of this book I have said good-bye to both my father and my husband. When I went to be with my dad at his deathbed, I read to him from a little journal I'd written and given to him on a Father's Day five years previously. It was filled with reasons I loved him. (He kept it on his desk.) One of the things I wrote was: "Dad—whenever I flew home, you were always at the gate." (This was in the days when you could still go to the gate to meet someone.) "I'd see your face searching for me, and then you'd see me and laugh, opening your arms for our great hug." The very last words I spoke to my dad

on this earth, and which I know he heard, were, "Dad—please, please—
be at the gate."

Will you endure the pain of a parting scene in order to give future
comfort? Will you go to the airport? Sit at the bedside of a dying friend?
And will you learn, from parting scenes, the value of expressing your
affection before a move or death prompts it?

One Last Story—Lee

Several threads from God's friendship pattern can wind their way
through every friendship, adding depth and beauty. I have told parts of
my story of my friendship with Lee in various Bible study guides, but here
is the complete version, beautifully illustrating many threads from God's
friendship pattern.

It began when we moved to Akron so that Steve could do a resi-
dency in orthopedic surgery. His hours were long and at night he was
weary. I was alone with two little boys and *craving* a kindred spirit.
When I went to the welcoming tea, for residents' wives, I was alert,
hopeful of meeting "her."

It was a hot August day, and sophisticated doctors' wives wearing
sundresses and sipping iced tea with lemon slices milled about. I
began to feel lonelier than ever. Many of the women had already
bonded and were talking animatedly. I'm not sure I would have even
gone back, but at the end of the tea the wife of a fourth-year-resident
stood up and said:

> Next week you'll have a chance to sign up for interest groups. Terri
> says she'll organize the tennis group, Mary will do quilting, and Lee
> is going to organize bridge. We need more—so if you are willing to
> organize something else—let me know! We'll pass around your sign-
> up sheet next week.

I drove home thinking I had been inspired with the perfect plan:

> I'll organize a beginner's Bible study! It will be so great. Women will
> come to Christ, they will lead their husbands to Christ, and their
> husbands will be physicians transformed by the love of Christ. They
> won't be about money or power, they will be about truly caring for
> the sick.

I was pumped. I also felt sure that a bonus would be that my kindred
spirit would be in that group.

I was excited to pass around the sheet the next week. I tried to make it sound as interesting as possible.

> Sign here for a beginner's study on Mark. Thursdays at 9:30.
> Babysitting. Coffee. A chance to meet new friends.
> 1.
> 2.
> 3.
> 4.
> 5.
> 6.
> 7.
> 8.
> 9.
> 10.

I watched the other sign-up sheets fill up. Ten for tennis, fifteen for bridge, seventeen for jazzercise ... and then, I saw mine. Except for me and a woman whom I knew was already a Christian, it was empty.

I drove home with some judgmental thoughts. *Well, Lord, I tried. Obviously these are just a bunch of worldly women. Uninterested in spiritual things. Hardhearted.*

And there, at a red light, came His still, small voice. Did you really try? How do you think you would have responded, before you knew Me, if a sheet like that had been passed around?

I knew I wouldn't have signed up. I would have been afraid of religious fanatics. I knew then that I needed to gain the trust of the women. I needed to, as the King James Version so quaintly puts it, "sh[o]w [myself] friendly" (Prov. 18:24). Ruth, Jonathan, and Mary took risks when they thought God was leading, "showing themselves friendly," and God rewarded them in many ways, including the gift of a wonderful friend.

Risk-Taking

I decided that I needed to join one of the other groups, "show myself friendly," and get to know the women. Then, maybe the next year there would be a few women who might sign up for Bible study. I had played bridge in college and had liked it. I felt a bit intimidated, being so rusty, but I thought I could go get a *Bridge for Beginners* book. I took a deep breath and dialed the name of the woman who was in charge: Lee Petno. We laugh now to remember her response. There were fifteen women who had signed up, and they needed a sixteenth. She said, "You are an answer to prayer!"

Greeting Scenes

The first meeting was at Lee's. I had enjoyed talking to her on the phone, and when she opened the door I remembered her from the tea: pretty, petite, and brimming with life. She enthusiastically welcomed me, repeated again how glad she was I had called, and put her arm around my waist warmly. I felt cared for. Lee had recently had a new baby—a little girl after two little boys. The women were all eager to see the baby, so I paraded into the nursery with them. There, bundled in a soft pink wrapper, was a tiny bundle with lots and lots of black hair and a little pink bow. "Ohhhh," I cried, entranced. Then, I said yearningly, "I want a girl!"

Lee said, "You have boys?"

"Two."

"I do too!"

"Wow!"

"I love my boys," Lee said. "They are such little men. But I think, whether she'll admit it or not, that every woman wants a daughter." She looked at her baby adoringly. "I'm *so* thankful to God."

I wondered, *Is Lee a believer?* As it turned out, she believed He existed, but didn't yet know how He longed to be personal to her, to show her that He is the rewarder of those who diligently seek Him. She *was* a faithful church attender, had a reverence for God, but she didn't yet have a love relationship with Him. Yet God was wooing her, and the birth of her daughter was part of His mercy to her. I was excited to realize, later, that the Lord had also actually called me to be part of His "wooing" of Lee.

As the year passed, I got to know Lee better. I still remember going to her house for tea alone and stopping spontaneously by the side of the road to gather wild daisies to take to her. There is the same kind of excitement in new friendships as there can be in a courtship. But for Christians, there is another amazing element. God may have planned the friendship. When we put our hand into the Lord's, and follow His lead, there is adventure around the corner.

Sharing Vulnerably

The following year, I passed around that sign-up sheet for Bible study again. *This* time Lee and three other wives from the bridge group signed up. Lee tells me now she thought I was a fanatic, always talking about Jesus, but still she was so unhappy, so discontent in her role as wife and mother that the topic we were studying—being a gracious woman— irresistibly drew her. Gradually, I saw Lee's defenses melt as God's truth moved like a healing balm over her heart. By the time we moved on to John's gospel, she was openly hungry like a baby bird with her beak wide open. How exciting it is to have a genuine seeker in a study whose questions reveal humility and vulnerability. She asked things like:

Jesus made the world? I didn't know that! I thought he began at Christmas! Is that what it is saying here?

I never knew the words "born again" were used by Jesus. I thought they were words fanatics made up. But here they are. What does Jesus really mean?

So you can't go to heaven without trusting Jesus. But what about the person who never hears about Jesus?

There is an excitement that people who are honest and vulnerable bring to others, which ignites excitement in the whole group. The other women became just as free, and one by one, we were seeing women changed by the power of God.

One of the first things she asked me was, "What about my husband? What if Vince doesn't believe? What if we have a divided house?"

We looked at Matthew 6:33 (Seek first His kingdom—and all these things will be added). We also studied 1 Peter 3, which gives wives of husbands "who do not obey the Word" hope. It says wives may be able to win their husbands without a word, by their pure and reverent behavior, by their quiet and gentle spirit.

Whatever You Ask Me to Do, I Will Do It

Lee was determined to obey the 1 Peter passage. She obeyed it *very* literally, not telling Vince one word about what had happened to her. (You actually *can* use words, but Peter's point was that our behavior should be the main communicator.) All she told Vince was that she was going to my Bible study. He began to see many changes in his wife, but poor Vince was mystified as to why Lee was so different.

When you are married to a resident, you've got to be flexible and it's challenging. Lee would work hard on a meal, light the candles, and anticipate a special family suppertime. Then Vince would call and say it would be another hour—then another—and usually, by the time he got home the meal was not steaming, but Lee was. She'd grab the leftovers from the fridge, throw them in the microwave, and slam them down in front of Vince, and then sit across from him, fuming.

But she was determined, through the power of Christ, to put off the old Lee and put on the new. No matter how late Vince arrived, no matter how many times he had changed his estimated time of arrival, Lee was gracious. The children were bathed and either ready for bed or in bed. When she heard his car in the driveway, she'd light the candles and greet him warmly with a kiss. The dinner would have been in a warm oven, and she'd place it gently on the table and sit across from him, smiling.

Vince was amazed. But Lee didn't tell him why.

One day when Lee was visiting me, she had car trouble. When Vince got home, he came over to help. As soon as this tall dark Italian man walked in the house, he looked at me and said, "Dee Brestin. Are you the one who is responsible for the change in my wife?"

I laughed. "No, that would be Jesus."

"Jesus!" He looked shocked. "Really!"

Soon after that my husband, Steve, invited Vince to a Bible study. It wasn't long before Vince put his trust in Christ.

An Intertwining of Intuition with Holy Spirit Power

One of the sweetest memories I have with my friendship with Lee has to do with the birth of our daughter Sally. Steve and I had been praying about having another baby. I longed for a girl, but Steve sensibly pointed out that God's plan might be for me to be the mother of three boys. I knew that was true.

Yet when Lee and I prayed, she encouraged me to pray for a girl. She pointed out that Jesus encourages us to ask. Of course I had to remember that God knew my needs better than I did and His best might be a boy— but it didn't hurt to ask for a girl.

When I was pregnant, I had a hunch—an intuitive sense—that God had said, "Yes." Steve and I had even planned to name our daughter Sara (after my sister) Lee (after Lee). "Sara Lee" was just too tempting to Steve, and he started patting my protruding tummy and saying, "Hey, Cupcake." I was afraid that nickname would stick, and that she might be pudgy, so, we reconsidered the name. We decided instead on Sally, and I told Lee to "hear the Lee in Sally."

In our Bible study group, I told the women we had asked for a girl and that I had a sense that God had said yes. They were so excited that they, in faith, threw me a baby shower for a girl! It scared me when they brought out a pink quilt they had made, each contributing a square. Lee's square had a pink baby buggy on it and a verse from Psalms. I thought, *What if I'm wrong? Will a bouncing baby boy shake the faith of these women?*

As the baby's due date approached, the doctor predicted a baby boy in early May. I said, "Steve and I have asked God for a girl on April 27."

He paused. "Really," he said, smiling. "Why April 27?"

"It's the only day Steve isn't working."

On April 27, I went into labor and our daughter was born. Steve cried, at the moment of birth, "God gave us a girl—and she looks just like me!"

I have a precious picture of Lee holding newborn Sally, thanking God for His goodness to us.

Dependence on God More Than a Friend

Steve and Vince ended their residences. That meant moves for both of us. Lee and I had to say good-bye. I remember the last night she suggested, "You want to have a slumber party?" I actually did, but knew we had to start our long drive to Seattle the next morning. Lee came over in the morning and we stood there, tears rolling down our cheeks. She hugged me, kissed baby Sally, and promised they'd try to come to Seattle to see us. We simply had to say good-bye. How clear it was that our trust had to be in Jesus, for He is the only One who will never betray you, never move away, and never die.

Unfailing Love

My friendship with Lee is now more than thirty years old. She's been there when I've needed her the most. Though we have never vowed friendship, we have been true to our "implicit vow." When Steve died, she asked me if it would bless me more for her to fly out for the funeral or later, when people weren't so attentive. I said, "I need you both times." She laughed, and agreed to both. The night before the funeral, I suddenly decided a song Steve had loved needed to be sung. It was a children's song—but how I remembered him unashamedly standing up with a big songbook, smiling, and enthusiastically leading a group of stouthearted men and smiling women in these lyrics:

> Happiness is to know the Savior
> > Living a life within His favor
> Having a change in my behavior
> > Happiness is the Lord
>
> Real joy is mine
> > No matter if teardrops start
> I've found the secret
> > It's Jesus in my heart ...

The night before the funeral I asked, "Vince—do you remember Steve closing our couples' Bible study each week with *Happiness Is the Lord?* I know this is so late—but I think Steve wants us to sing it. Could you possibly find it and lead the congregation in it tomorrow morning?"

Grinning, Vince pulled a piece of paper out of his shirt pocket. "Got the lyrics from the Internet." He laughed at my shocked look. "I thought you might want them."

Before Vince introduced the song, he told the eight hundred guests, which included many doctors and nurses who did not know the Lord, how Steve had impacted him. "My name is Vincent Petno. I am a cardiologist who could fix other peoples' hearts, but I couldn't fix my own. And then I met this man named Steve Brestin. He lived differently from the other doctors I'd known.

"One day I found out why. Steve knew that happiness was to know the Savior." Then Vince and my sons led the congregation in that simple child's song—they were completely off-key, but I know it was a sweet sound in heaven. I could almost see Steve's radiant face watching through the veil. Lee and I smiled at each other through tears. Unfailing love, like that of the Lord.

My Parting Scene with You

The Lord has taught me some profound truths about friendship, and I hope that His teachings have flowed through me to you, my reader, and now my friend. So we are bound together in His truth and in His Spirit. It's painful to close this book; it's hard to say good-bye, but I am encouraged by C. S. Lewis's great shout, "REMEMBER! CHRISTIANS NEVER SAY GOOD-BYE!"[4] I will meet every one of you who has personally trusted Christ for her salvation—one day, in eternity!

So I ask you to go in peace and to practice, as I will, God's friendship pattern. God promises us that, as we obey His Word, His love will truly be made complete in us (1 John 2:5). We will experience greater and greater fellowship with one another (1 John 1:7) and we will become Christ's reflection in the world. I am coming to understand, more and more, what the apostle John meant when he said, "For we realize that our life in this world is actually His life lived in us" (1 John 4:17 PH).

In His Unfailing Love,
Dee

NOTES

Chapter 1: From Girlhood On, Gifted for Intimacy

1. Elliot Engel, "Of Male Bondage," *Newsweek,* June 21, 1982, 13.
2. Janet Lever, "Sex Differences in the Games Children Play," *Social Problems,* 23 (1976): 478–87.
3. Zick Rubin, *Children's Friendships* (Cambridge, Mass.: Harvard University Press, 1980), 108.
4. Rosalind Wiseman, *Queen Bees and Wannabes* (New York: Three Rivers Press, 2002), 18.
5. Paul D. Robbins, "Must Men Be Friendless?" *Leadership,* Fall 1984, 26.
6. Richard Cohen, "Men Need Liberating from Repressed Feelings," in *Male-Female Roles* (St. Paul, Minn.: Greenhaven Press, 1983), 96.
7. Joel D. Block, *Friendship—How To Give It—How To Get It* (New York: MacMillan, 1980), 57, 80.
8. Lillian B. Rubin, *Just Friends: The Role of Friendship in Our Lives* (New York: Harper and Row, 1985), 63.
9. Ladd Wheeler, Harry Reis, and John Nezlik, "Loneliness, Social Interaction and Sex Roles," *Journal of Personality and Social Psychology* 45 (1983): 951.
10. Meredith Bedgas, "Why Women are the 'Most Wanted,'" *Ladies Home Journal,* March 2005, 20.

Chapter 2: Women Are Friendlier

1. Joel D. Block and Diane Greenberg, *Women and Friendship* (New York: Harper and Row, 1985), 3.
2. Lillian B. Rubin, *Just Friends: The Role of Friendship in Our Lives* (New York: Harper and Row, 1985), 105.
3. Stuart Miller, *Men and Friendship* (Boston: Houghton Mifflin, 1983), 2.
4. C. S. Lewis, *The Four Loves* (San Diego: Harcourt, Brace, Jovanovich, 1960), 90.
5. Sondra Enos, "A New Kind Of Father," *Ladies Home Journal,* June 1986, 47.
6. Rubin, *Just Friends,* 161.

7. Deborah Tannen, *You Just Don't Understand: Women and Men in Conversation* (New York: William Morrow and Company, 1990), 77.

8. Doreen Kimura, "Sex Differences in the Brain," *Scientific American,* May 13, 2002, Sidebar.

9. Ibid.

10. James Wilson, *The Marriage Problem: How Our Culture Has Weakened Families* (New York: HarperCollins, 2002), 188.

11. Judith Blakemore, "Children's Nurturant Interactions with Their Infant Siblings: An Exploration of Gender Differences and Maternal Socialization," *Sex Roles: A Journal of Research,* (1990): 43–57.

12. Barbara Eakins, R. Gene Eakins, *Sex Differences in Human Communications* (Boston: Houghton Mifflin, 1978), 67–69.

13. Dr. Donald Joy as interviewed by Dr. James Dobson, Cassette #CS099, "The Innate Differences Between Males and Females" (Broadcast of "Focus on the Family" from Arcadia, California).

14. "Just How the Sexes Differ," *Newsweek,* May 18, 1981, 78.

15. Joy, "The Innate Differences."

16. Gary Smalley on "Focus on the Family" Broadcast from Arcadia, California, on September 29, 1986.

17. Dr. Gabriele Lusser Rico, *Writing the Natural Way: Using Right-Brain Techniques to Release Your Expressive Powers* (Boston: Houghton Mifflin, 1983), 69.

18. Lori Andrews, "How Women Think," *Parents,* April 1986, 74.

19. Rico, *Writing the Natural Way,* 78.

20. Paul Tournier, *The Gift of Feeling* (Atlanta: John Knox Press, 1981), 29.

21. Ibid., 27.

22. Ibid., 27–28.

23. Anna Kuchment, "The More Social Sex," *Newsweek,* May 10, 2004.

24. Andrews, "How Women Think," 74.

25. Tim Hackler, *Biology Influences Sex Roles* (St. Paul, Minn.: Greenhaven Press, 1983), 17.

26. Ibid.

27. Ellen Goodman and Patricia O'Brien, *I Know Just What You Mean* (New York: Simon and Schuster, 2000), 57.

28. Joy, "The Innate Differences."

29. Ibid.

30. Kuchment, "The More Social Sex."

31. Smalley, Focus on the Family broadcast.

32. Dr. Seuss, *Horton Hatches the Egg* (New York: Random House, 1940).

33. Elliot Engel, "Of Male Bondage," *Newsweek,* June 21, 1982, 13.

34. Hackler, "Biology Influences Sex Roles," 17.

35. Marian Sandmaier, "When a Woman Smiles, Nobody Listens," *Mademoiselle,* July 1986, 139.

36. Carol Gilligan, *In a Different Voice: Psychological Theory and Women's Development* (Cambridge, Mass.: Harvard University Press, 1982), 10.

Chapter 3: The Darker Side of Being Crazy-Glued

1. Eva Margolies, *The Best of Friends, the Worst of Enemies* (New York: Doubleday, 1985), 16.
2. *Detroit Free Press*, March 3, 1966.
3. Rachel Simmons, *Odd Girl Out* (New York: Harcourt, Inc., 2002), 30.
4. Rosalind Wiseman, *Queen Bees & Wannabes* (New York: Three Rivers Press, 2002), 24–48.
5. "Advice: My Best Friend?" *Psychology Today,* March–April 2004.
6. C. S. Lewis, *The Four Loves* (San Diego: Harcourt, Brace, Jovanovich, 1960), 113.
7. Alexandra Robbins, *Pledged: The Secret Life of Sororities* (New York: Hyperion, 2004).
8. Vanessa Juarez, "Sisters' Keeper," *Newsweek,* April 15, 2004.

Chapter 4: Relational Idolatry

1. Dr. Jane Flax as interviewed by Eva Margolies, in *The Best of Friends, the Worst of Enemies* (New York: Doubleday, 1985), 83.
2. Dr. John Stott has an excellent article explaining why a lifelong and loving homosexual partnership is not a Christian option in *Christianity Today*, November 22, 1985.
3. Andrew Seu, "Born That Way," *World Magazine*, November 6, 2004, 55.
4. Maxine Hancock and Karen Mains, *Child Sexual Abuse* (Wheaton, Ill.: Harold Shaw Publishers, 1987), 38.
5. Karen C. Meiselman, *Incest: A Psychological Study of Causes and Effects with Treatment Recommendations* (San Francisco: Jossey Bass, Inc., 1978), 188.
6. Lori Thorkelson Rentzel, *Emotional Dependency: A Threat to Close Friendships* (San Rafael, Calif.: Exodus Int'l, 1984), 3.
7. Ibid.
8. John White, *Eros Defiled: The Christian and Sexual Sin* (Downers Grove, Ill.: InterVarsity Press, 1977), 120.
9. Ibid.
10. Darlene Bogle, *Long Road to Love* (Grand Rapids, Mich.: Zondervan, 1985).
11. There are many active ministries available for the person who longs for release and help in overcoming homosexuality. They have newsletters, cassettes, and retreats.

Help for Those in the Bondage of Homosexuality
www.settingcaptivesfree.com
This free ministry provides a wonderful online Bible study
for those in the bondage of sexual or food addictions.

Desert Stream

P.O. Box 9999

Kansas City, MO 64134

816-767-1730 (phone)

866-359-0500 (toll-free)

Andy Comiskey, Director

www.desertstream.org

Desert Stream offers a newsletter and a wide range of support groups, conferences, and seminars as well as an outreach to AIDS victims.

Exodus International

P.O. Box 540119

Orlando, FL 32854

407-599-6872

www.exodus-international.org

Exodus International provides recommendations of ministries throughout the country and other information for homosexuals.

Spatula Ministries

Mrs. Barbara Johnson

Box 444

La Habra, CA 90633

www.oneway.jesusanswers.com

Spatula Ministries offers help to parents and families of homosexuals.

Chapter 5: Cinderella in the Change of Life

1. Collette Dowling, *The Cinderella Complex* (New York: Summit Books, 1981), 110.
2. Pastor John Bronson, Guest Speaker's Sermon to the Evangelical Free Church of Kearney, Nebraska, June 1986.
3. The Targum, *Clarke's Commentary* (Nashville: Abingdon, 1824), 192.
4. Bronson, Sermon, June 1986.
5. Luci Shaw quoted in an interview by LaVonne Neff, "The Meaning of Faith in the Face of Death," *Christian Life,* June 1986, 44.
6. Luci Shaw, "Beauty for Ashes," *Christian Life,* June 1986, 44.
7. Daniel Levinson quoted in an article by Steven Hamon, "Closer Than a Brother," *Christianity Today,* Jan. 1, 1982, 31.
8. Dr. Beth Hess, "The Good a Friend Can Do," *Changing Times,* April 1981, 63.
9. Dr. Joel D. Block and Diane Greenberg, *Women and Friendship* (New York: Franklin Watts, 1985), 4.

10. Bronson, Sermon, June 1986.

11. Jan Titterington, "Insights from the Book of Ruth," *His,* January 1976, 3.

12. Block and Greenberg, *Women and Friendship,* 29–30.

13. Titterington, "Insights," 3.

14. Hans Christian Andersen, "The Snow Queen," in *Fairy Tales* (New York: Grosset and Dunlap, 1981).

15. Dr. James Dobson, *What Wives Wish Their Husbands Knew About Women* (Wheaton, Ill.: Tyndale House Publishers, 1975), 143.

Chapter 6: Binding Up the Brokenhearted

1. Pastor John Bronson, Guest Speaker's Sermon to the Evangelical Free Church of Kearney, Nebraska, June 1986.

2. Ibid.

3. Paula D'Arcy, *Song for Sarah* (Wheaton, Ill.: Harold Shaw Publishers, 1979), 162.

4. Carin Rubenstein, Ph.D., and Margaret Jaworski, "When Husbands Rate Second," *Family Circle,* May 5, 1987, 105.

5. Barbara Eakins, R. Gene Eakins, *Sex Differences in Human Communication* (Boston: Houghton Mifflin, 1978).

6. Jay Adams, *Competent to Counsel* (Grand Rapids, Mich.: Baker Book House, 1970), 140.

7. Louis McBurney, "Treatment for Infidelity Fallout," *Leadership,* Spring 1986, 113.

8. Ibid.

9. Lorraine Hansberry, *A Raisin in the Sun* (New York: New American Library, Inc., 1958), 125.

Chapter 7: The Risk of Love

1. Luci Shaw, "Perfect Love Vanishes Fear," in *Listen to the Green* (Wheaton, Ill.: Harold Shaw Publishers, 1971), 40.

2. Randolph Bourne, *Youth and Life,* quoted in "Celebrating Friendship," *Saturday Review,* October 1961, 6.

3. Gordon MacDonald, *Ordering Your Private World* (Nashville: Thomas Nelson, 1984), 105.

4. C. S. Lewis, *The Four Loves* (San Diego: Harcourt Brace Jovanovich, 1960), 103.

5. Ann Kiemel Anderson and Jan Kiemel Ream, interviewed by Rebecca Powell Parat, "Our Search for Acceptance," *Christian Life,* March 1986, 26–30.

6. Gail MacDonald, interviewed by Ruth Senter, "Joined Hands in Ministry," *Partnership,* January/February 1984, 54.

7. Kevin Sullivan, *Anne of Green Gables,* DVD, directed by Kevin Sullivan (Burbank, Calif.: Pid, 2001).

Chapter 8: Best Friends

1. L.M. Montgomery, *Anne of Green Gables* (Boston: L.C. Page and Publishers, 1940), 75.
2. Lillian Rubin, *Just Friends* (New York: Harper and Row, 1985), 63.
3. Ibid.
4. Dr. Donald Joy as interviewed by Dr. James Dobson, Cassette #CS099, "The Innate Differences Between Males and Females" (Broadcast of "Focus on the Family" from Arcadia, California).
5. Letha Scanzoni, "On Friendship and Homosexuality," *Christianity Today,* September 27, 1974, 11.
6. Thornton Wilder, *Our Town,* in *Three Plays* (New York: Harper and Row, 1938), 100.
7. Dee Brestin, *Finders Keepers* (Wheaton, Ill.: Harold Shaw Publishers, 1983).

Chapter 9: Unfailing Love

1. Lesley Dormen, "Good Friends Are Not Like Family," *Glamour,* September 1986, 162.
2. Lillian Rubin, *Just Friends* (New York: Harper and Row, 1985), 175.
3. Anita Moreland Smith, "My Sister, My Friend?" *Today's Christian Woman,* Nov./Dec. 1986, 41.
4. Ibid., 42.
5. Walter Wangerin Jr., *Mourning into Dancing* (Grand Rapids, Mich.: Zondervan, 1992), 93.
6. Ibid.
7. Mary Brown Parlee, "The Friendship Bond," *Psychology Today,* October 1979, 43.
8. Eva Margolies, *The Best of Friends, the Worst of Enemies* (New York: Doubleday, 1985), 148–49.

Chapter 10: Roses and Alligators

1. Kristen Johnson Ingram, *Being a Christian Friend* (Valley Forge, Pa.: Judson Press, 1985), 61–62.
2. Gini Kopecky, "Betrayals (Just Between Friends)," *Redbook,* September 1983.
3. Dawson Trotman, as quoted by Gordon MacDonald in *Ordering Your Private World* (Nashville: Thomas Nelson, 1984), 106.
4. Ingram, *Being a Christian Friend,* 63.
5. Madonna Kolbenschlag, *Kiss Sleeping Beauty Good-bye* (New York: Doubleday, 1979), 58.
6. Karen and David Mains, "Don't Give Me That Guilt Trip" (Wheaton, Ill., *The Chapel of the Air,* Tape 648a).
7. Mary Alice Kellogg, "When True-Blue Turns Green," *Savvy,* May 1986, 28.

Chapter 11: God Knows Our Needs Better Than We Do

1. Luci Shaw, "Yes to Shame and Glory," *Christianity Today,* Dec. 12, 1986, 22.
2. Ibid.
3. Isabel Anders, "The Unexpected Gift," *Partnership,* Jan./Feb. 1984, 42.
4. Ibid.
5. Ibid.
6. Ibid., 43.
7. Dorothy Pape, *In Search of God's Ideal Woman* (Downers Grove, Ill.: InterVarsity Press, 1976), 27.
8. Walter Wangerin, Jr., as quoted by Bruce Buursma, *Chicago Tribune,* Aug. 8, 1986.
9. Gary Smalley, John Trent, *The Blessing* (Nashville: Thomas Nelson, 1986), 24–25.
10. Shaw, "Yes to Shame and Glory," 23.
11. Ibid.
12. Ibid., 22.

Chapter 12: The Mentor Relationship

1. Win Couchman, "Cross-Generational Relationships," speaking at Women for Christ, 1983, Winter Break (tape available from Domain Communications, Wheaton, Ill.).
2. Jill Briscoe, "Woman Power," tape #7 (tape available from Bible Believers Cassettes, Springdale, Ark.).
3. Karen Mains, "An Interview with Karen Mains: Our Search for Spiritual Mentors," *Virtue,* October 1985, 73.
4. Couchman, "Cross-Generational Relationships."
5. Linda Phillips-Jones, *Mentors and Protéges* (New York: Arbor House, 1982), 37.
6. Ibid., 40.
7. Dr. James Dobson, "Turn Your Heart Towards Home" film series.
8. Briscoe, "Woman Power," tape #3.
9. Couchman, "Cross-Generational Relationships."
10. Ibid.
11. Mains, "Spiritual Mentors."

Chapter 13: Reflections of Christ

1. Luci Shaw, "Salutation," in *The Secret Trees* (Wheaton, Ill.: Harold Shaw Publishers, 1976), 32.
2. Ann Kiemel Anderson and Jan Kiemel Ream, interviewed by Rebecca Powell Parat, "Our Search for Acceptance," *Christian Life,* March 1986, 26–32.
3. William Shakespeare, *Romeo and Juliet,* Act 2, Scene 2, in *Great Books of the Western World,* vol. 26 (Chicago: Encyclopedia Britannica, Inc., 1952), 296.
4. Sheldon Vanauken, *A Severe Mercy, Davy's Edition* (San Francisco: Harper and Row, 1977), 230.

READERS' GUIDE

For Personal Reflection or
Group Discussion

READERS' GUIDE

One of the first threads introduced from "God's Friendship Pattern" is "Parting Scenes and Greeting Scenes." It seems God often zooms His camera in at these poignant moments, for they tell us so much. As we consider these scenes, you will also see other threads this book mentions.

1. Remembering that Naomi has lost her whole family, have someone read the parting scene in Ruth 1:8–18. What do you learn about Naomi from this scene? About Ruth?

    A. Why do you think Naomi's daughters-in-law were weeping? Can you share a moment from a personal parting scene where you were very sad, but are glad for the memory of words expressed? If so, share briefly.

    B. Explain Shakespeare's words: "Parting is such sweet sorrow."

    C. In chapter 1, Dee talks about "small partings." How can even these partings be made more meaningful?

    D. What have you learned about parting scenes that you think you might use?

    E. What risks do you see Ruth taking here? Why do you think she took them?

2. Have someone read the greeting scene between David and Jonathan in 1 Samuel 18:1–4. Describe and comment on the scene.

    A. What did Jonathan know about David that might have caused him to be so drawn to him?

    B. At the end of chapter 7, Dee talks about the importance of seeking out "poets and giant slayers," friends who will help us grow. What are some qualities in these people and how might you discern them when you initially cross paths?

C. What kinds of risks did Jonathan take in befriending David? Have you ever taken a risk in friendship? If so, describe it and the outcome.

D. How might Jonathan's friendship have been a provision of God for David?

3. Have someone read the parting scene between David and Jonathan in 1 Samuel 20:41–42.

A. How do you see Jonathan helping David to part from him?

B. Do you have any friends who really help you find strength in God? What is it about them that encourages you?

C. When Kenneth Taylor originally paraphrased this scene for *The Living Bible*, he portrayed them as sadly shaking hands. Dee gave examples in chapter 2 of how men are often fearful that their friendships will be misunderstood as being homosexual. In what ways are you thankful that you and your friends feel relatively free to express yourselves?

4. Have someone read the greeting scene between Mary and Elizabeth in Luke 1:45–49. Describe and comment on the scene.

A. It was important to Mary to take this seventy-mile journey to see Elizabeth. Why, do you think?

B. At the opening of chapter 12, Win Couchman defines a mentor. What is her definition and in what ways do you see Elizabeth qualifying?

C. How did Elizabeth's prophetic greeting help Mary find strength in God?

5. In chapters 3 and 4, Dee discusses relational idolatry. What is relational idolatry and what are some warning signs?

6. In chapter 9, Dee talks about implicit vows. Why did she recommend them over outspoken vows, and how do you know if you have an "implicit vow" with a friend?

7. Share one or two concepts that you believe will stay with you from this book. What are they and why are they meaningful to you? (Hear from as many as would like to share.)